Grab the Extinguisher, My Birthday Cake's on Fire!

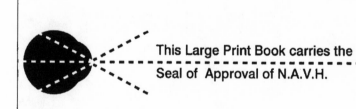

This Large Print Book carries the
Seal of Approval of N.A.V.H.

Grab the Extinguisher, My Birthday Cake's on Fire!

Growing Older Gracefully and Other Such Things

Patricia Lorenz

Thorndike Press • Waterville, Maine

Published in 2005 by arrangement with Guideposts Book Division.

Thorndike Press® Large Print Senior Lifestyles.

The tree indicium is a trademark of Thorndike Press.

The text of this Large Print edition is unabridged.
Other aspects of the book may vary from the original edition.

Set in 16 pt. Plantin by Elena Picard.

Printed in the United States on permanent paper.

Library of Congress Cataloging-in-Publication Data

Lorenz, Patricia.
    Grab the extinguisher, my birthday cake's on fire! : growing older gracefully and other such things / By Patricia Lorenz.
    p. cm.
    Originally published: Carmel, N.Y. : Guideposts, c2004.
    ISBN 0-7862-7426-3 (lg. print : hc : alk. paper)
    1. Aging — Religious aspects — Christianity. 2. Older Christians — Religious life. 3. Christian life — Humor. 4. Christian life — Anecdotes. 5. Large type books. I. Title.
BV4580.G72 2005
  242′.65—dc22
                                    2004029034

Dedicated to all the members
of the SWILL gang, Southeastern
Wisconsin Interesting Ladies League,
which has been meeting at my house
since it began in 1989;
and to the BAG Ladies,
my writer friends scattered
across the United States.
Thank you all for giving me
encouragement, hope
and plenty of life-saving laughs
that have sent me into middle age
and beyond hooting and
celebrating all the way.

As the Founder/CEO of NAVH, the only national health agency solely devoted to those who, although not totally blind, have an eye disease which could lead to serious visual impairment, I am pleased to recognize Thorndike Press★ as one of the leading publishers in the large print field.

Founded in 1954 in San Francisco to prepare large print textbooks for partially seeing children, NAVH became the pioneer and standard setting agency in the preparation of large type.

Today, those publishers who meet our standards carry the prestigious "Seal of Approval" indicating high quality large print. We are delighted that Thorndike Press is one of the publishers whose titles meet these standards. We are also pleased to recognize the significant contribution Thorndike Press is making in this important and growing field.

Lorraine H. Marchi, L.H.D.
Founder/CEO
NAVH

★ Thorndike Press encompasses the following imprints: Thorndike, Wheeler, Walker and Large Print Press.

Contents

Chapter Two

Ribbons, Bows and Wrapping: Enjoy Life's Surprises

Chapter Three

Party Time! Participate in Life's Celebrations

Chapter Four

Pin the Tail on the Donkey:
Make Light of Embarrassing
Moments 95

Chapter Five

The Birthday Cake: Get the Most out of Life 124

Chapter Six

Say Cheese! Treasure Special Memories 157

Chapter Seven

Chapter Eight

Chapter Nine

Introduction

Patricia Lorenz has packed quite a bit of living into fifty-eight years. This book is a celebration of her life and, in turn, our lives. It's about growing older gracefully and staying young at heart.

Pat has been a friend of Guideposts since 1982, when she wrote her first story for us, "The Smock," about her mother's well-worn shirt that was playfully exchanged between the two of them for years in a love-filled game. Since then, Pat has contributed to the devotional book *Daily Guideposts* and is the author of several books, including *Life's Too Short to Fold Your Underwear*.

In this exclusive collection, we've chosen those articles that best epitomize Pat's spunkiness and storytelling skills. She travels back and forth in time, remembering and celebrating different moments of her life. As a successful single parent of four now-grown children, she has learned over the years what is important and what isn't.

Family, they're key. So, too, are friends,

freedom, adventures, hard work, playtime, goals and dreams, health, and most importantly faith in God. This is the important stuff in life, the things that count, and by sharing her experiences with us, we all come away with a richer understanding of this gift called life.

With every chapter, she also serves up bite-sized Scripture, which is the foundation of her faith and which keeps her grounded.

Of course, you can't have a party without "Invitations," and that is what Pat does in the first chapter of this entertaining gathering. She invites us to do something new, whether it's following Grandma and Grandpa Knapp's no-stress, no-fuss example of drop-in hospitality or creating a "love fund" box for those times when others are in need.

Then we focus on how to enjoy life's surprises in "Ribbons, Bows and Wrapping." Pat delights in her son Andrew's unexpected placement of a Baby Jesus figurine, and she discovers a commonality in her parish and a neighboring Lutheran church.

"Party Time! Participate in Life's Celebrations" takes us to birthday parties and weddings, lets us rejoice in the sounds of Christmas, and acknowledges life's achievements and quieter times.

We're all susceptible to embarrassing moments or occasions when we're not at our best, and Pat doesn't sidestep hers. In "Pin the Tail on the Donkey," she makes light of those instances and reveals lessons that contribute to her "graceful aging." It's when we can laugh at ourselves or forgive ourselves that we're on the right track.

In "The Birthday Cake," Pat dishes out stories that reveal that little something extra about herself that brings her joy. Whether it's asking the question, "Am I really happy doing this work?" or recognizing how to overcome SAD (seasonal affective disorder) by looking for the light, Pat tells us how to get the most out of life.

After we've stuffed ourselves silly with cake, we'll move on to those Kodak moments in "Say Cheese! Treasure Special Memories." From "brown cows" with the folks to Pat's education with the Sisters of Loretto, from first dates to the first grandchild, memories add a sweetness to life that is unmatched.

What's a party without gifts? "Presents" is about how to receive gifts of love, and "Party Favors" tells us how to pass on kindness — two similar yet distinct facets of living a happier life.

And after the celebration is done, what's left is the "Post-Party Cleanup: Age Gracefully and Stay Young at Heart." Here Pat reflects on those who've reached their golden years and those who've passed away. She takes stock on how hard we work and why, and she talks about prayer. It always comes back to that — our conversation with God.

So welcome! Pull up a chair and visit awhile. And share in the celebration of this gift called life.

— The Editors of Guideposts Books

Chapter One

Invitations
Do Something New

Get into the habit of inviting
guests home for dinner or,
if they need lodging, for the night.
ROMANS 12:13 (TLB)

You can't have a party without friends, so Patricia Lorenz is inviting you to her celebration of life! RSVP, and you will be captivated by the stories of love and service that have motivated and moved Pat to an understanding of the best in people.

Grandma and Grandpa Knapp's drop-in-anytime hospitality is how Pat runs her household now, photos on the fridge remind her to pray for family and friends on a daily basis, a local deejay inspires Pat to create a "Love Fund" for neighbors hit by tragedy, and haircuts allow her to get to know her son's friends in a different kind of way.

Don't let the party go by. Pat is waiting for you!

Drop-In-Anytime Hospitality

During the 1950s when I visited Grandpa and Grandma Knapp in Blandinsville, Illinois (population six hundred), I was amazed at the number of drop-in visitors they had. In the winter, they'd visit in front of the coal stove that plunked and hissed in the middle of the living room. In the summer, neighbors walked over to sit a spell in the porch swing. Grandma would bring out the pitcher of lemonade and an extra chair or two from the dining room, so everybody could sit down.

Every day they came: old farmer friends who'd retired like Grandpa and moved into town, shopkeepers on their way home from work, the preacher from the local church, the town librarian.

In 1998, when my youngest child went off to college and my home became an empty nest, I wondered what had happened to that custom of drop-in-anytime hospitality. Why is it that we think we need a week to prepare for guests, and that we must have every nook and cranny in our homes white-glove-inspection clean, and that we must feed our visitors elaborate meals every time they come to visit?

I decided right then to encourage everyone I knew to stop in anytime. Whenever I saw my friends or neighbors or acquaintances, I'd say, "Stop in anytime! I mean it. If my car's in the garage, I'm home. So stop in."

Well, people started doing it. Now, three or four times a week I get a surprise visit from someone. I'm not expected to have the house clean or food prepared. Usually I just boil water for tea, pour lemonade and pass out graham crackers, if that's all I have on hand. And without all the stress and fuss, my guests and I can just visit our fool heads off, enjoying every glorious minute.

Kitchen Cabinet Philosophy

Four quotes in bright colors and varying sizes are taped to my kitchen cabinets. The first quote, on a piece of shocking pink paper, says in huge black letters, GET OVER IT. STOP WHINING AND START WINNING. That quote wakes me up every morning and reminds me to hold no grudges and maintain a positive attitude all day long.

Quote number two is on the cabinet over the counter that holds seventy jars of tea. It says, IF YOU'RE COLD, TEA WILL WARM YOU. IF YOU'RE HEATED, IT WILL COOL YOU. IF YOU'RE DEPRESSED, IT WILL CHEER YOU. IF YOU'RE EXCITED, IT WILL CALM YOU (BRITISH PRIME MINISTER WILLIAM GLADSTONE). That quote reminds me to be hospitable and invite my friends over for tea often. I do, and my little tea parties have enriched my life immeasurably over the years.

The next quote, the one taped to my kitchen cabinet just to the right of the kitchen sink, spells out four of the most important sentences I can say: I AM PROUD OF YOU. WHAT IS YOUR OPINION? I LOVE YOU. THANK YOU. These four sentences nudge me to be a more affirming, affectionate, appreciative and positive person. I tried to punctuate my conversations with those four sentences when my children were growing up.

The last quote, to the left of the kitchen sink, typed on bright yellow paper, proclaims, IF YOU HAD FAITH EVEN AS TINY AS A MUSTARD SEED, YOU COULD SAY TO THIS MOUNTAIN, "MOVE!" AND IT WOULD GO FAR AWAY. NOTHING IS IMPOSSIBLE (MATTHEW 17:20, TLB). That's the one that gives me constant hope, unlimited encouragement and a daily dose of comfort, no matter what I'm trying to accomplish.

So there you have it — a whole philosophy of life on my kitchen cabinets. And if you're ever in Oak Creek, Wisconsin, stop in for tea. The kitchen's always open!

Refrigerator Prayers

You can tell a lot about a person by looking at the front of his or her refrigerator. My seventy-nine-year-old stepmother Bev has magnets on hers from some of the countries she and my dad have visited over the years.

My busy son Michael and his wife Amy have large magnetic alphabet letters at the bottom of their refrigerator for their little ones, Hannah, Zachary and Chloe, to practice their spelling words. My friend Sharon has hundreds of tiny magnetic words on her refrigerator, so her whole family can create sweet, goofy or sentimental poems.

My refrigerator reminds me to pray a dozen times a day because the top two-thirds of it is a solid mass of four-by-six-inch photos. Everyone from one-hundred-year-old Great Aunt Peggy and ninety-five-year-old Aunt Helen to my seven beautiful grandchildren. My four children, their spouses, my folks, brother, sister, their families, other aunts, uncles, cousins and assorted friends all hold a place of honor on my refrigerator.

One is a picture of Jane Knapp, a friend I've never met in person. She interviewed me by telephone on her small radio station years ago, and we struck up an immediate friendship. In the year 2000, Jane's e-mails were gut-wrenching updates about her cancer. One day, after months of chemo, I received this note from Jane:

"The doctor called a few minutes ago and told me that the PET scan results showed new cancers in my liver, kidney and lung. He said usually new cancers do not pop up at the same time, so I'm very discouraged but have to keep believing in the power of prayer."

Jane's photo and all the others on that frequently opened door help keep my loved ones in my mind, heart and prayers many times a day, every day.

How to Link Up a Prayer Chain

A prayer chain is a line of communication among believers who are willing to be "on call" to pray for a specific need. The setup allows urgent requests to be relayed immediately without waiting for the pastor to announce them at the Sunday service; one phone call activates the network.

One spring years ago, my own church started a prayer chain and I had occasion to use it almost at once. My husband at the time was sent to the hospital with a wildly fibrillating heart. With all those people praying, we felt the power of their caring lift us above our fear.

Since then, I've talked to prayer-chain organizers of various denominations — Methodist, Baptist, Lutheran, Catholic. With only minor variations, their groups are set up in the same way.

1. Locate at least two "anchorpeople" to head up the network. It's a good idea to have more than one person in charge in case one can't be reached or is on vacation. Publish these names in your weekly church bulletin and ask volunteers to get in touch with them. Your pastor and Sunday school teachers can make announcements, too.

2. Divide into teams. Make a master list of volunteers' names and phone numbers, then divide them into groups small enough to allow the full chain to be activated in a reasonable time. For example, if you have a hundred people willing to pray, separate them into eight or ten teams, each with a captain.

3. Have a simple format. Give each person in the chain a list of phone numbers for his or her team. When one of the anchorpeople gets a prayer request, he or she calls the other anchor. Each then calls half of the team captains who, in their turn, call the first person on their teams. That person calls the second one, and so on. If someone isn't home, the caller skips to the next name and tries later to reach the one who was missed. Last person on the list notifies the captain of the

team that the full team is functioning.

4. Keep phone contact brief. Prayer-chain calls should be quick and efficient. The person receiving the call should listen carefully, repeat the request to make sure he or she understands it, hang up, and call the next person on the list.

5. Pray at once, in your own way. It doesn't matter where you pray or what you say. Getting in touch with God is the important thing. Some people are most comfortable with a traditional prayer, such as the Lord's Prayer or a favorite Bible reading. Others prefer to make up a prayer or to meditate quietly.

That's all there is to it. Updates on a specific situation are optional. But usually people on the chain appreciate hearing if there is a change in the need or an answer to prayer. Your pastor may be willing to include a report in his or her weekly announcements.

Whether you're linked at the sending or receiving end of a prayer chain, I think you'll find it's a very good connection.

Saying Grace

When I was a kid, whenever my Uncle Ralph visited, he'd end each meal by saying something at breakneck speed that he'd been required to say at military school years before: "My gastronomical satiety admonishes me that I have reached that state of deglutition consistent with dietetic integrity." After a few visits, he laughingly admitted that all it meant was "I'm full."

As a parent, I started thinking about the formalized, memorized grace my family said before meals. We rattled it off without listening to the words as quickly as Uncle Ralph blurted out his "I'm full" message.

I decided to forego the memorized version and instead let the children take turns saying whatever came to mind. Sometimes it was thoughtful, as when Jeanne said, "God bless Grandma and help her to feel better. Thank You for this food, our home and each other." Sometimes it was quick and filled with teenage humor, like the time Michael blurted out, "Rub-a-dub-dub, thank You for the grub. Amen."

Before meals is the perfect time you and your family can draw close to one another and to God.

Love Fund

Larry the Legend, a flamboyant radio announcer in Milwaukee, invited his listeners to call in and "speak your opinions . . . tell it like it is." Many called and complained about inflation, job layoffs, rising crime and government waste. Larry heard tragic personal stories: an old woman robbed for the fifth time in a year; a young widow with three small children who lost her paycheck; or a fire or crime victim who could barely face another day. Periodically Larry started a radio "Love Fund," so his listeners could aid these people with money, clothing, food and sometimes even places to live.

After listening to Larry help these people, I decided to start my own "Love Fund." I simply placed a large cardboard box in a closet where I put usable clothing, toys, bedding, housewares and canned goods. There was even a Bible or two in there, purchased for a song at the local Goodwill store or rummage sales.

Whenever we heard of another family who suffered a tragedy — a house fire perhaps, wreckage from a tornado or an out-of-work breadwinner — we packed up suitable items from the big "Love Fund" box and delivered it as a family project.

My children didn't even mind cleaning

out their closets, drawers and desks occasionally because they knew their outgrown clothes and toys would be put in the "Love Fund" box, and eventually be used and enjoyed by another boy or girl.

Be Prepared

A man sitting in the chair next to my desk at work suddenly slumped over to the floor. I jumped up, tried to take his pulse, then put my ear to his mouth. He wasn't breathing!

I'd taken a course in cardiopulmonary resuscitation a few years earlier, but now I was terrified. A man was dying in front of me! Muttering a quick prayer for help, I began a steady rhythm of heart massage and instructed an office worker to hold the man's nose and breathe into his mouth each time I said, "Now!" Before the ambulance arrived, the man started breathing. I was still shaking when I thought about what would have happened to him if I hadn't taken that CPR course.

Come to think of it, I've taken plenty of courses: a baby-sitting class when I was a teenager, first aid, swimming classes, senior lifesaving, childbirth classes, even a home safety class. I know that if we have faith in the Lord, He'll take care of us. But

I also believe that He depends on us to master the worldly problems by being prepared.

This year I'd like to take a basic auto mechanics class in case my car ever breaks down on the highway. How about you? Are your swimming skills up to par? Ever had CPR? Perhaps a refresher first-aid course. . . .

A New Way of Listening

I received a phone call the other day from a telephone salesperson trying to sell me symphony tickets and obviously reading the long pitch off a card.

I usually handle telephone sales calls in one of four ways:

1. Hang up on them mid-sentence.
2. Let them finish their spiel and then politely decline.
3. Buy something I really don't want because I don't know how to say *no*.
4. I purchase the product joyfully because it's a good idea or a nice value.

It's funny, but sometimes those are the four ways I find myself listening to sermons at church:

1. Some Sundays I find myself "hanging up" on the sermons completely. My mind wanders and I think of other things.
2. Sometimes I listen, but at the end I decline politely by ignoring the message — and the Word of God.
3. Still other times I accept the words and their meaning, but once I get home I never quite figure out what to do with them.
4. I am a joyful listener who absorbs the Word of God and happily puts it to good use in my daily life.

At church, I'm going to try harder to listen more carefully and joyfully and with more acceptance of God's Word. And at home I'm going to put those words to good use. Will you join me?

Grandma Barbara

When Jeanne, my oldest child, was born, she had five living grandmothers: two grandmothers and three great-grandmothers, all of whom adored her. But when Andrew, my youngest child, was born ten years later, none of his grandmothers was alive. Of course, when my dad married Bev, she became an "instant" grandma — but they live three hours away.

Years ago, an older woman who lived in Wyoming called me when she was visiting friends in Milwaukee. She said she had read my devotionals in the book *Daily Guideposts* and wanted me to know that she also was a single parent who had raised two boys and two girls alone. We started to correspond by letters and phone. Once Barbara sent me flowers when I was having a bad week. After she had eye surgery and was feeling depressed, I insisted that she spend a few weeks with us. We had a wonderful time — and she showered Andrew with lots of hugs, great stories and devoted attention.

You know, the senior retirement homes are full of older people who enjoy being active and have time to give of themselves. There are probably many who attend your church, who perhaps live alone and would love to be "grandma" or "grandpa" to your children. Our "Grandma Barbara" came back for another visit a few months later, and Andrew and I visited her in Cheyenne that summer.

It's not hard to find a grandma or grandpa if you need one. And it's not hard to provide grandchildren to those who need them.

Clippers, a Cowlick and a Cut

Right after fifteen-year-old Andrew talked me into practically shaving his head at the beginning of the summer, he talked two of his friends into doing the same thing. Safety in numbers, I presumed.

"Please, Mom, Brian and Paul really want you to cut their hair like mine. School's out. It'll be cool!"

I looked at the boys, each sporting sun-streaked, four-inch-long haircuts. "It's okay, Mrs. L. Shave it off!"

I insisted they call their parents for permission, and then for the next hour I ran my electric clippers over each head until just an eighth of an inch of fuzz remained. During each haircut, I got to know my son's friends much better. I became very well acquainted with Paul's two stubborn cowlicks, and as we talked about school and his part-time job, I gained a new respect for his hard work at the tree nursery. When I nicked Brian's ear, I made noises over him like a mother hen, then heard about his plans for the future and about his family. His gentleness and quiet sense of humor impressed me.

That night after the boys left, Andrew asked, "Mom, do you like my friends?"

I'd never told my son what I thought

about any of his friends; not Paul, Brian, Nick, Dave, Bert, Tracey, Heather, Tiffany or Cheryl. I sat down with Andrew and went down the list, pointing out what I thought were the best qualities of each: Bert's friendliness, Tracey's bubbling personality, Heather's openness, etc.

Throughout that school year, Andrew's friends filled our home with their infectious laughter, constant chatter and empty stomachs. And by its end, they had become my friends, too.

One New Friend Per Week

Years ago, I worked for a large radio-TV station that employed more than three hundred people. Every day I saw the same faces in the halls, yet I knew less than half of them by name.

At a Christmas party one year, I got to know one of the reporters. I learned that he and his wife were expecting their first child. We talked about our jobs; Ron learned a little about writing radio commercials and I learned a little more about the newsroom. Afterward, whenever we saw each other in the hall, we stopped and chatted or gave a friendly wave.

It was then I decided to learn the name

of one person I worked with every week. Then when I saw them in the halls, I could address them by name with a comment like, "You sounded great on the air this morning." Or, "I heard TV sales are up. Congratulations!" Or, "What's new in the newsroom?" A new friend every week. Doesn't that sound like a marvelous way to spend a year?

Out Loud Compliments

A few years ago, in a column by Ann Landers, I read a letter from someone who had been viewing an art exhibit among hundreds of strangers. Suddenly, a young woman approached her and said, "You are a beautiful lady." The older woman was thunderstruck, saying in her letter to Ann:

> I am eighty-eight years old and never considered myself anything special to look at. But I'm healthy and happy and grateful to the good Lord for all His blessings. Maybe this is what comes through in my face. Every day this week I have been cheered by that lovely compliment.

After I read that, I asked myself, "Why shouldn't we compliment strangers?" I often see someone in a crowd who is inspiring — an older man with a wonderful smile, or a harried young mother who treats her children with respect in a difficult situation, or someone who's extra friendly in the grocery line. But actually to compliment a stranger out loud? I didn't know if I could do it.

A few weeks later, when I was at the beauty shop getting a haircut, I took a deep breath and said to the woman next to me, "You have such beautiful hair and that style looks so good on you."

The woman, who was about my age, beamed. We started talking, and before long discovered we were practically neighbors and knew some people in common. Now, whenever I see her around town, we smile and exchange greetings. We're no longer strangers. We're friends.

The SWILL Gang

I'd closed the curtains in my family room, flipped the TV channels and settled into my green rocker for another night alone when the phone rang. It was a woman named Sunny calling from Valdosta, Georgia.

"I just read something you wrote in *The Single Parent* magazine and I have to talk to

you. I'm a single parent, too, and sometimes I just don't know if I can make it on
my own. I thought it would help to talk to
someone else who's raising children alone."
We talked for an hour that night, and then
Sunny called every couple of weeks.

A few months later Sunny told me she
wanted to move back north, so I invited
her to Milwaukee for a weekend to attend
a conference for single people. She stayed
for a week and bought a house while she
was in town. She kept calling me her best
friend even though I was wallowing too
deep in my own miseries to be anybody's
best anything. That year, 1989, was the
worst of my life, and I just was not up to
helping someone else solve her problems.

In fact, I needed someone who would
listen to my own problems. And they were
many. The man I'd dated for ten months
suddenly moved to Oklahoma to start a
new career. Harold, my ex-husband, died
of leukemia, not long after he had married
his girlfriend on the day our divorce was
final. Our nine-year-old son Andrew was
devastated by his father's death, but I was
too angry about the whole divorce thing in
the first place even to know how to grieve.

That same year my twenty-year-old
daughter Jeanne got caught in the middle

of the California earthquake, and I lived through nightmarish days until I learned she was safe. And my eighteen-year-old daughter Julia, after graduating from high school, decided to spend the summer before college testing my sense of "loving motherhood." We hollered and picked at each other all summer. I wondered if I just couldn't get used to the idea of first Harold, then Jeanne and now Julia leaving me. Many nights my family room felt like an empty auditorium as I sat alone with the TV set. *Lord,* I wondered, *what has happened to my family? Will this room ever seem full again?*

Then, as a favor to Sunny, after she made the move to Milwaukee with her two young daughters, I decided to gather some of my women friends to meet her. I called every woman I knew: friends from church, work, the neighborhood. Friends I met over the years through other people. Mothers of my children's friends. One from my writing club.

I was a bit nervous at first, inviting them to my house all at once, knowing that few of them knew one another. When they arrived I introduced everyone, and before long we were talking, laughing and gabbing like old friends about our jobs, children and lifestyles. Sunny was delighted. In fact, she said, "You people are downright interesting!"

Tina piped up, "I think we should do this every month! It can be our club. We could call it the Southeastern Wisconsin Interesting Ladies League! S-W-I-L-L."

I laughed. "SWILL? We're going to form a club and call it SWILL?"

"Why not?" Sharon asked. "We can gather together, unload all the swill that creeps into our lives, and get support from one another."

So we began at the end of 1989. We decided to meet at my house every month since I have the largest family room and the fewest family members to uproot on Friday nights.

We kept it simple. SWILL would have only one rule: confidentiality. Whatever problems or heartaches discussed in that family room during our SWILL meetings would stay in that room. We would trust one another, care about one another, and help one another if possible.

Over the years at least twenty-five women have woven their way in and out of SWILL. Anyone can bring an interesting friend to the meetings, and if that friend likes us she can become a regular. Sometimes we've had a dozen at one time, and other months, because of hectic schedules, we've had only three or four.

As we got to know one another, we began to care more and more about each other. We became a family. I never worry about cleaning the house before a SWILL meeting because nobody's there to do a white-glove inspection. And I don't worry about fancy refreshments. If one of us is having a chocolate or salty foods craving, she brings a bag of candy or pretzels to toss on the coffee table to share. But we resolved from the beginning never to get bogged down, as some clubs do, with a fancy food complex.

SWILL welcomes everyone regardless of age, race, religion or occupation. Everyone from Carrie, a young married woman in her late twenties with four small children, struggling with the possibility of her marriage ending, to Eunice, who's been married for forty-two years and taken enough college-level classes in her retirement to be one of the most interesting people in the group.

When one of our group, Linda, died of heart failure at age thirty-nine after meeting with us only a short time, we mourned together. Later we discussed ways to solve the medical insurance problems that often face single, overstressed parents, like Linda, who must work as many as three jobs to make ends meet.

When Jody's teenage son Daniel died in a car accident, we held one another and cried with Jody at the funeral.

When Gail, whose children were starting college, went back to school to study nursing, we spent hours talking her into staying in school when she wanted to quit. One of our members, a counselor, helped Gail through some test anxiety problems one night. Gail graduated in May, and we all took a bow.

When Barb's son came home from Desert Storm and moved back into her and her husband's "empty nest," and then a few months later her daughter moved back home with her husband and new baby, we listened to the ups and downs of Barb's five-adults-in-one-house, three-generation family. We gave her lots of advice, including that it was okay for her to go back to work full-time.

Carol, whose happy marriage rubs off on all of us, points out that even a happy marriage isn't perfect all the time, but that a sense of humor can get you through most of the swill that marriage can dish out.

Sunny benefited tremendously from

SWILL. She became more independent, found a wonderful job in the Milwaukee school system, made lots of new friends at work, in her neighborhood and in her church, and moved on to start her own support network.

What did SWILL do for me, the one who was simply trying to find a few friends for Sunny? I think I'm the one who benefited most. These women — single, separated, divorced, married, from all walks of life — opened their hearts and their lives to me, month after month. They listened to me, laughed with me and helped me through the rough times. When I had three children in college at once and a twelve-year-old at home, they helped me even more through the struggles by offering financial advice as well as emotional help. I've learned to talk about my fears and my failures, and to admit that I'm scared at times and that it's okay to have conflicts with the ones you love.

I've also learned how important it is to get out of the house and get plenty of exercise. Gail and I started roller-skating two or three times a week on the bike path near Lake Michigan. And Betsy and I fast-walked every Saturday morning for an hour. I lost thirty-five pounds and never felt better physically in my life!

One thing's for sure: 1990 and '91 were better years by far than 1989 because of the interesting and loving women friends I made through SWILL. And now? Well, I'm just wondering if we shouldn't change our name to SWELL. Because we are. A swell bunch of women who have become a family to one another, a nonjudgmental support system that's always there on the first Friday of the month.

Once again the good Lord has filled my family room with "family." A new family of friends. It's amazing how much love I feel now that I've learned to open up my life to these friends and to nourish that friendship on a regular basis.

Get Out and Vote

The first Tuesday of November is the most important day of the year for our country, states, cities and towns. It's the day "we, the people" are able to decide how our government will run, based on which candidates we choose to put in office.

Though I'm not a very political person publicly, I do try to read up about the issues. I talk about them at home and discuss them with friends whose opinions I value. Then I make my decision. And I always vote.

And I always took my children with me to the polling place. My youngest son Andrew would go right into the booth with me, pull the red lever to close the curtain and watch intently to see whom I was going to help put in office. The next day he was as anxious as I was to see which of "our" candidates won.

Our children can only learn how democracy works from us. So it's important that we teach them about freedom of choice and the democratic process not only by what we say, but also by what we do. If there are children in your family, talk about the issues and candidates with them. Take them with you when you vote. And most of all, do get out and vote.

Extra Service Done with a Smile

For thirty years my dad worked as a mail carrier for the U.S. Postal Service. His daily fifty-mile route, mostly on country gravel roads in northern Illinois, always doubled its mail volume during the two weeks before Christmas. Dad worked long hours those weeks and came home exhausted, but I never heard him complain.

45

When Dad retired, I heard from some of his elderly patrons that during those Christmas weeks he would walk up their long country lanes, through two or three feet of snow, to deliver the mail right to their door, rather than leave it in the box at the end of the lane. Sometimes he would trudge up those lanes on foot to hand-deliver an eagerly awaited letter from a son overseas. Or he would leave a large package inside a front porch rather than propped up against the mailbox in the snow.

Extra service done with a smile . . . that was the way Dad carried on the business of delivering the mail during those hectic holiday weeks.

No Excuses

Years ago I complained to an old high-school friend that with four children at home I couldn't find the time to write letters in my Christmas cards. (I'm one of those people who hates to get Christmas cards with nothing but the sender's signature inside.)

My friend looked me straight in the eye and said, "Why, the best thing that ever motivated me was *having* four children at home! I learned to make time for those things that were important to me. I learned to do personal projects — like writing, sewing, painting, cooking — in twenty-minute blocks."

From that day on I stopped using my children and the hectic hustle-bustle of the season as an excuse. I started writing those Christmas letters to my faraway friends and relatives. I'd take an hour while Andrew, a preschooler at the time, watched *Sesame Street*. I wrote letters to Aunt Bernadine and cousin Mary Beth in the car while waiting to pick up Michael from basketball practice and drum lessons. Sometimes I used the kitchen counter while the roast was cooking and Julia was practicing cheerleading in the living room.

That year I wrote more than three dozen letters. It was a good feeling to learn that if I really want to do something, I *can* find the time.

This year I'm going to find time to read the books of Psalms and Proverbs. What are you going to do?

Christmas Day Miseries

After a movie with my friend Dianne, I went home. The house was dark and empty when I got there. The children were spending the day with their father . . . it was his turn. I'd forgotten to fill the wood burner before I left and the family room was cold. I sat there and simply gave in to a wave of loneliness and despair on that Christmas Day of 1987.

Since then I've avoided the "Christmas Day miseries" by planning ahead with friends to spend the day at each other's homes. And occasionally it's arranged that the kids split the day so both parents can be included. I'm also on the lookout for other single parents whose children "take turns" with the ex-spouse or other adults who will be spending the day alone, and I include them in my festivities.

You don't have to look far to find adults who might be spending Christmas Day alone. Invite them over — and it might take a forceful invitation to get them out of the house. Turn on the lights, the music . . . and don't forget to pile wood on the wood burner.

Have a Merry Christmas! I insist on it!

Mourn Awhile

One day while looking through a folder of old newspaper clippings, I pulled out an article about the deadly tornado that ripped through the small town of Barneveld, Wisconsin, killing nine people and destroying nearly every home and business in the village.

The reporter wrote, "The wind took almost all of St. Mary's Catholic Church, but it left part of page 168. The wind tore it from a hymnal and pinned it to the ground with a chunk of pew. Page 168 is a song: 'O Come and Mourn with Me Awhile.' "

I wondered if that small piece of paper from the hymnal was God's gentle, loving touch, reminding the people of Barneveld that it was all right to lose themselves in grief and sorrow — momentarily. It was as if God were saying, "Cry for a while, then get on with the business of rebuilding your lives."

I, too, had been mourning, lonely and depressed for two years over the fact that my marriage had ended. After I read that article about the tornado, I decided that I'd mourned long enough. It was time to approach life with a positive new outlook. I made some new friends, joined a group of single parents, started teaching a college copywriting class, made an effort to have special moments or hours alone with each of my four children every week, created a daily morning quiet time with God, and tried to approach each day with hope and determination.

How about you? Have you taken the time to mourn — *awhile?* Now it's time to get on with the business of rebuilding. With God's help you can do it, too.

The Conquest of Fear

The day dawned with another month of Milwaukee's blustery cold weather ahead. I was out of wood for the wood burner. I'd never split logs or used a chain saw before, but we certainly needed the wood. Could I do it?

I was afraid to use the heavy, sharp equipment. Finally, I heaved the heavy ax down over my head and slammed it into one log after another on the chopping block. Most times I missed the log completely. My shoulders ached, my hands shook. But two hours later there was a pile of wood ready to be cut to sixteen-inch lengths with the chain saw.

Terrified that I would cut through the electric cord or myself, I started the chain saw. Sawdust blew everywhere . . . on my neck, in my face. I worked on, sweating, aching. A blister developed on my thumb, and the pain in my lower back brought me to tears.

Oh, God, where are You.

Several hours later, the wood pile was re-stocked . . . and I learned something more valuable than how to work a chain saw. I learned that with determination and inspiration I can do anything. Anything! Christ on the Cross gave us all the inspiration we need.

Is there something in your life that you're afraid to attempt because you don't think you can? In Basil King's classic *The Conquest of Fear*, he says: "Be bold, and mighty forces will come to your aid."

The "Perfect" Mate

I've been single since 1985. In the following years, I've met and dated a number of different men, always looking for the "perfect" mate. But usually I only dated each one once or twice because they just weren't perfect enough. And they've left me wondering if the perfect mate really exists.

Then one day a friend suggested I put my family room to good use by letting that be the monthly meeting place for a women's group. After that, I made an effort to bring other people into my home, both male and female. I joined a few organizations, changed careers, helped start a

Bible study group at church, worked hard at keeping the relationships with my married friends, and started visiting relatives and friends all over the country.

Oh, I still have those days when I wonder if God has someone perfect out there for me. But instead of feeling like part of me is missing, I make the effort to keep my life full by making sure it's filled with people. Today, I can honestly say that I'm enjoying the single life. In fact, I can't ever remember being happier!

Chapter Two

Ribbons, Bows
and Wrapping
Enjoy Life's Surprises

Thanks be to God for his inexpressible gift!
II CORINTHIANS 9:15 (RSV)

Surprises can appear quickly or reveal themselves gradually. In "Ribbons, Bows and Wrapping," Patricia Lorenz regains energy and joy from a parade of a thousand dancing women, and delights in the unexpected placement of a Baby Jesus figurine. There are more stories that will show you how to enjoy the fancy dressings in life. Just turn the page for these delightful packages of life's surprises.

Water Slide Glee

There's an old saying that goes, "I hear and forget. I see and I remember. I do and I understand."

One hot summer day during the early eighties, my nine-year-old son Michael ran into the house out of breath. "Mom! There's a new water slide at the park! It's really fast, and there's a tunnel and everything!"

I'd never seen or heard of a water slide before, and what he was trying to describe was as foreign to me as molecular biology. But a few days later Michael and I went to the water slide together. We both screamed with delight as we plopped down on our bellies at the top and experienced heart-stopping speed as we slid down the wet, four-story-tall slide with its bobsledlike tunnels and hairpin turns. Suddenly, I understood what Michael had been trying to tell me and, to tell the truth, I couldn't wait to understand it again.

Before that experience I'd been afraid of two things: giving up my old typewriter to join the computer age, and taking a trip by myself. After that experience with Michael, I decided I shouldn't be afraid to try anything new. After all, I might like it as much as I liked the water slide! And you know what? I did! I've been computer literate since 1982. And I've taken many trips by myself, and every one was a fabulous experience.

Yes!

One night a few days before Mother's Day 1999, I was in a bit of a whiny, poor-me mood. I e-mailed my brother and sister-in-law, telling them that none of my four children (who all lived out of town or state) could be with me on Mother's Day, so on Sunday I was planning to go in-line skating by myself along Milwaukee's beautiful lakefront. "I'm going to go where no one will recognize me and where I can pretend I'm an old spinster who never had any children," I joked.

A few hours later, Linda called to say that she was going to Japan the day after next to meet Joe, who would be on a five-day layover there on his job as an airline pilot. They wanted me to join them, at very little cost, because Linda works for another major airline and we'd be flying on standby passes.

She was giving me thirty-six hours notice to drop everything and fly to Japan, only the second time in my life I'd be off the continent! My first reaction was to rattle off all the things I had to do that week. But then I caught myself. I shouted, "Yes!" did a happy dance around the house, canceled or postponed everything on my calendar, and started packing.

The trip, the sightseeing, the food and the people were fabulous! But what I will always remember most is not only was I able to say *yes*, I did say *yes* to an outrageous opportunity and learned once again that *yes* is not only magical, it's almost always a great idea.

The Thousand Dancing Women of Narita

I'm so glad I traveled to Japan in 1999 with my brother Joe and sister-in-law Linda. One day, after visiting a breath-takingly beautiful temple and seeing some of Japan's amazing parks and gardens, we stopped for a sit-on-the-floor lunch at a small restaurant nestled among the shops on a winding, busy street in the small town of Narita.

As we finished our meal, we heard drums pounding and music playing in the street. We looked up to see rows and rows of women dancing in perfect unison, all wearing festive black and white kimonos with different colored sashes.

We quickly paid our bill and stepped out onto the street to catch what we figured would be the tail-end of a short parade. But instead, the happy procession continued. Row after row of women of all ages — arms and legs moving in unison to the music — danced past us. The magnificent parade went on for at least thirty minutes.

"Where are they going?" I asked a shopkeeper.

"They're going to the temple. Once a year all the women in the town process to the temple in this way."

As I watched the women, joy on their faces and a bounce to their perfectly choreographed steps, I started to feel a little guilty. *I've never ever felt that happy on my way to church back in Wisconsin,* I thought.

When the parade of women was over, we walked through the market shops where Linda and I each purchased a lovely cotton kimono. Now, whenever I see it hanging in my closet or slip it on over my shoulders, I try to pursue everything I do that day with a little more energy, a little more excitement and a little more joy. Just like the thousand dancing women of Narita on their way to the temple.

An Ecumenical Spirit

My parish, St. Matthew's Catholic Church in Oak Creek, Wisconsin, only offered basic religion classes for middle schoolers on school nights. Andrew had too heavy a homework load during the week to attend their classes so, wanting my son to be in a weekly Bible study, I enrolled him in a neighboring Lutheran church's morning Sunday school class.

Even though I was raised in a Catholic family and educated for fourteen years by the wonderful Sisters of Loretto, I've always felt blessed with an ecumenical spirit.

That year, while Andrew was at Sunday school, I attended the church's Bible study group that met there at the same time. When classes were over, we headed for St. Matthew's to attend Mass. In addition to learning a lot about the Bible from both Pastor Jim and Intern Kathy (who was about to be ordained), I learned just how much our two churches had in common. But most importantly, I learned that it's okay to be a little unorthodox in my search for godliness.

A Matter of Focus

During a two-week hospital stay, I grew very fond of my grandmotherly roommate Agnes. One day while she was napping, I noticed that on the stand beside her bed she had propped up a strip of needlepoint with an odd kind of design on it. Later, when she was awake, I asked her about it.

"A friend made that for me. Can you see what it says?"

I shook my head. "What do you mean? It's some foreign language, isn't it?"

"No," replied Agnes with a wide grin. "It's a word you've seen and spoken all of your life."

For the rest of the day, I glanced at the design off and on, but I did not see the word — only meaningless white ciphers.

"It'll come," Agnes reassured me. "Just keep looking at it."

The next morning when I woke up, I turned to the design. *Jesus.* The word stood out in bold brown letters. "I don't know why it took me so long," I said to Agnes. "It's so obvious."

"Well," Agnes said, her eyes twinkling, "don't feel bad. Sometimes it takes folks a lifetime to find Jesus."

"But once you've found Him," I said, smiling back, "your life is in focus."

Two Friends of Mine

Let me tell you about two friends of mine.

The first is Bill Lombardo. I met him on the BART (Bay Area Rapid Transit) train heading for San Francisco. He's in his early fifties, a musician, married twenty-seven years, with two children. He used to play in his Uncle Guy Lombardo's band. You've heard of *him,* right? Then Bill started his own fifteen-piece orchestra, eleven musicians and four singers. Bill was in my home state of Wisconsin only once that he can remember, years ago when he spent the night with a friend in the tiny town of Cuba City. Well, when Bill told me that, I couldn't believe it. You see, that very day, my son Michael, also a musician, was moving to Cuba City (population 1,200) to take over the high-school band director's job! Bill and I had a lot to talk about.

My other friend is Vivian Su, born in Canada of Chinese descent. She's sixty-seven years old, but looks and acts fifty. That's because she fast-walks a mile and a half around the lake in Oakland, California, every morning for exercise. Vivian and her husband have visited China twice, climbing the Great Wall both times. A fascinating lady who loves to shop, I met her in the bargain basement of a department store the same week I met Bill.

So what's so unusual about my friends Bill and Vivian? Well, I only knew them for twenty minutes each, Bill on the BART train and Vivian in the bargain basement. We just started talking, and before I knew it, I felt like I did have new friends.

I'll tell you one thing: Bill and Vivian sure perked up my visit to California. I remember the conversations I had with them in greater detail than I remember Golden Gate Park or Chinatown.

Emilio, Andrew and I

When my son Andrew was thirteen, we took a twenty-seven-day trip across America with a family friend. Just outside Salt Lake City, we climbed Timpanogos Mountain, so we could take a cave tour at the top.

After the tour, when we stepped into daylight for the hour-long hike down the narrow, steep mountain trail, we were greeted with dark skies and rain. I insisted on waiting for Emilio, a frail gentleman in his seventies whom we had met on the tour. He said it had taken him more than two hours to make what was normally a one-hour climb up the mountain, and I was worried he would have trouble getting down in the rain. Suddenly, lightning sliced through the rocks ahead of us. The thunder, which sounded like ten thousand bullwhips snapping into the rocks all around us, was terrifying.

Andrew screamed, "Mom, hurry! We

have to get out of here! Please, Mom! Let's go! Hurry up!"

Knowing that Emilio needed help and that Andrew's fear of the storm needed to be calmed, I convinced my son to let Emilio, whose knees were hurting, hold on to Andrew's shoulders as we inched our way down that slippery path. When the rain let up, we started to sing. We talked. We whistled. Emilio taught Andrew some Spanish.

For three and a half hours on that steep, slippery path, Andrew and Emilio were glued to each other, the older man's hands on Andrew's thirteen-year-old shoulders. When we reached the bottom and said good-bye to our new friend, I asked Andrew if he had learned anything that day. He answered simply, "*Yup*. I learned that when you help somebody, you forget your own fears."

A Gradual Process

Even though major-league baseball isn't my favorite pastime, I jumped at the chance to take my son Andrew to a Milwaukee Brewers game in July 1999. Just four weeks earlier he'd had surgery. He hadn't been out of the house except for short walks and, quite frankly, I was getting impatient with him.

At Milwaukee County Stadium that night, we watched the game, we watched the people, we ate junk food. Then suddenly, just after the seventh-inning stretch, around 9:30, there was a power failure and the enormous lights that lit up the field suddenly went out. The stadium and field were left in a hazy darkness, and within a few minutes all the players retreated into the dugouts.

Because the score was Milwaukee 10, Kansas City 3, many people got up and left for home. Others blew bubbles, headed for the refreshment stands or sang songs in groups. I finally pulled a book out of my backpack and started to read under the few dusky lights that were still on in the grandstand.

Twenty minutes later, when I looked up to see that the field was aglow with bright lights once again and the game was ready to resume, I couldn't believe my eyes. I hadn't even noticed when the lights came back on. Andrew said they'd come on very gradually over the entire thirty-minute period.

Gradually, huh? They went from total darkness to bright enough to play ball and I hadn't even noticed?

I started to think about Andrew's healing. He'd gone from major surgery to cheering for the Brewers in four weeks and I hadn't really noticed that he'd been getting a little better each day . . . gradually. I'd been too concerned about pushing him to exercise harder, sleep less, take fewer pain pills, do a few chores and call his friends to notice that he was walking tall, eating normally and anxious to get out to see his beloved team.

Let There Be Light!

Even though I don't do a lot of cooking, I'm in the kitchen a few hours every day, usually at the counter, reading mail, paying bills, writing letters, talking on the phone or watching the news. Ever since we moved into this house, I've wished that the kitchen ceiling light was brighter. The fixture would only allow sixty-watt bulbs, and as my fiftieth birthday and a new eyeglass prescription loomed, I decided it was time to "light up my life."

I brought home a huge light fixture that held four four-feet-long fluorescent bulbs. After my dad installed the thing, we had our first ceremonial "turn on." Light bounced off the walls, from window to door, ceiling to floor. There was light everywhere! It made me so happy that I couldn't wait to get up in the morning to turn it on.

At the same time, another area of my life was as dreary as my kitchen had been: my faith. Oh, I went to church every Sunday, said my daily prayers and even taught Sunday school to high-school sophomores. But my faith wasn't growing.

Then I read in our church bulletin that Father Ron was starting an adult Bible study class. I decided to go. As we made our way through the Gospel of John, I felt my faith grow brighter and stronger as I gained new knowledge of God's Word.

I only wish I'd done this earlier! Now I can't wait to get up each morning and turn on my faith, too.

Motorized Mother

"I'm tired of spending my whole life in that car," I grumbled, scowling as I grabbed the car keys off the kitchen counter. My son Michael had just reminded me that we had to go out to buy his basketball shoes that evening.

"I'm averaging two hundred miles a week just driving you kids to games, lessons, rehearsals, shopping, cheerleading practice, religion classes and taking you to friends' houses! Two hundred miles a week and nobody cares!" My voice faded when I realized nobody was listening.

As a single parent, I was the one to do the driving whenever the four kids needed to be driven somewhere around Oak Creek, Wisconsin's sprawling twenty-eight square miles.

"Mom, don't forget there's the dance at school tonight," Julia reminded.

Back home from that jaunt, I collapsed in front of the TV to read the newspaper, when suddenly six-year-old Andrew was at my side. "Mommy, can we go to the store now?"

"No, dear, not now," I said wearily.

"But your birthday's tomorrow," Andrew whimpered.

Ah yes, my birthday. I'd forgotten I'd promised to take him shopping. He'd been saving his nickels and dimes to buy me a present. He'd decided upon earrings and expected me to help pick them out.

"All right, Andrew," I said. "Let me put my shoes back on and get ready. We'll go now." How do you say no to such a big heart implanted in such a little body?

At the store we browsed among the

carousels of earrings, giggling at the strange ones, *oohing* and *aahing* at the beautiful ones. Andrew pointed to a pair he liked. I told him they were beautiful. (They were also on sale for three dollars, a dollar less than what he had clutched in his cowboy coin purse.)

Knowing he'd made up his mind, I said, "Andrew, decide what you want to do while I go over here and buy socks for Michael." I knew he needed to be alone.

From the next aisle I could hear his pride-filled voice saying, "Yes, please," when the lady asked him if he needed a box for the earrings. "It's my mom's birthday and I'm going to wrap them in red paper with white hearts."

After a stop for an ice cream cone, we headed home, and Andrew disappeared into his room with the red paper and a roll of tape.

"Get your pajamas on, honey. Then come to my room and we'll read your bedtime story in my bed."

When he jumped in the bed, Andrew snuggled close to me.

"Mommy, this is the happiest day of my life!"

"Why is that, honey?"

"It's the first time I've ever been able to

do anything for you!" Then his arms surrounded me in a spontaneous bear hug.

While Andrew plodded out loud through one of his first-grade readers, I thought about my own acts of giving. I was always giving to my four children — especially behind the wheel of that car. Yet somehow I was never really happy about it.

Later I tucked this little boy with the big heart into his bed. "What about prayers, Mom?"

I'd forgotten. "Oh, of course, honey."

I held Andrew's small hands in mine and thanked God for my small son — and for all my children. I asked God to help me be a happier, more cheerful mother.

Later I looked up the verse that had been running through my head, the one about God loving a cheerful giver (II Corinthians 9:7).

Then and there I decided to stop being such a grouch about all the driving. And as I became a cheerful chauffeur — something I thought I'd never be — I found that I was listening to things I'd never quite heard before. On the way to band practice or drum lessons, Michael, age fourteen, thought out loud about whether he should go out for football. He also told me about the girl in his class who had called him the night before, discussed whether he should get a job after school and talked about what he wanted to do with his life.

When Julia, age fifteen, was in the car with me, she bubbled on and on about the latest antics in her cheerleading squad, about the boy who'd asked her to homecoming, about the student council fundraiser and about getting extra help in geometry.

On the way to Jeanne's piano lessons, confirmation classes and a special event downtown at the Milwaukee High School of the Arts, where she was a senior, we talked about where she wanted to go to college, what was happening in her art classes and why she felt her social life was at a standstill.

Amazed by what I'd missed as a cranky mom honking and griping her way around Oak Creek, I began looking forward to wheeling around town with my four kids in tow. Given a chance, the kids opened up. We laughed together, debated, questioned, shared our feelings and grew much closer. I still drove two hundred miles a week, but I looked forward to every mile, because driving time became family time in our car. Prime time. Time for giving cheerfully.

Motorcyclists and a Minister

The newspaper picture showed a large group of surly-looking motorcycle riders perched on their big "hog" cycles, with an elderly man in front of them, his right arm raised as if to protect himself.

My immediate reaction was, *That poor guy didn't stand a chance! Those weirdos probably mugged him, then laughed as they gunned their engines and raced off.*

Then I read the caption beneath the picture. "About two hundred and fifty bikers gathered Sunday to picnic with friends while waiting to have their motorcycles blessed by a Lutheran minister."

Next time I saw a group of black-leather-jacketed motor-cycle riders whizzing past me on the street, instead of cowering or scoffing in disapproval, I smiled and waved. Know what? They smiled, waved back and went on their way.

Bonus Times

After church one Sunday, I had the whole rest of the day to myself and I blew it!

Andrew, eleven, was visiting a friend, so it was just me, a glorious, sunshiny October day in Wisconsin and all the time in the world to do whatever I wanted. I could have gone to downtown Milwaukee to a performing arts festival or invited a friend to join me at a crafts fair at our local zoo. I could have taken a walk along Lake Michigan just two miles from my house and searched for beach glass. I could have even taken advantage of the peace and quiet to curl up with a good book. The list of beautiful things to do was endless!

What did I do? I turned on the TV to a football game and fell asleep on the couch. And I don't even like football! When I woke up, I moped around the house, groggy, out of sorts and sorry for myself. I had wasted my entire afternoon.

The next morning I noticed a plaque on an office wall:

Man shall be called to account for every permitted pleasure he failed to enjoy.

So now I've decided: There's work. There's rest. There's free time for social interaction, brisk exercise, intellectual stimulation, or quiet solitude in which to read, pray or just think. And then there are *bonus* times — sometimes precious whole days — that are simply gifts. Whether planned or unexpected, they're my very own *to-do-with-whatever-I-want* time "to account for a permitted pleasure."

My vow? Next time a bonus day comes my way I'll be prepared. I'm going to find one of God's "permitted pleasures" and enjoy myself with abandon.

Composing Christmas

As a radio copywriter, I often started writing Christmas commercials in September with words like, "Order now for the coming holiday season" or "Avoid the Christmas rush" or "Just in time for your holiday gift giving."

By November, I often found myself muttering, "Bah humbug!" Bitterly, I thought, *Why does Christmas have to be such a long, drawn-out mega-merchandising affair?*

Then I read something by Dr. Earl Count, an American scholar, who defined Christmas as:

A spontaneous drama of the common folk, a prayer, a hymn. All the while that Raphael was painting the Sistine Madonna, Frenchmen were building the Cathedral of Chartres, English Bishops composing the Book of Common Prayer, Handel his Messiah, Bach his

B-Minor Mass . . . the common people, out of whom these geniuses sprang, were composing Christmas.

And what a composition it turned out to be! From the lighting of the first candle on the Advent wreath to the celebration of the arrival of the wise men, Christmas really is the most amazing time of year.

So when the materialism of the season started to get me down, I thought I'd create Christmas for others by giving a food basket to a needy family, or driving a shut-in to a Christmas concert, or filling little stockings with holiday treats and handing them out in the children's wing of the local hospital.

What can you do to give Christmas to another?

Jesus in the Bread Box

In preparation for Advent, I asked nine-year-old Andrew to set up our manger scene. He carefully unwrapped the delicate, hand-painted animals, shepherds, wise men, Mary and Joseph, and placed the Baby Jesus in the wooden manger. The next day I noticed Baby Jesus was missing. *Andrew's playing a joke on me,* I thought.

Later, when I started fixing supper, I opened the bread box on the kitchen counter and there was Baby Jesus next to the bread! When I asked Andrew about this, his explanation was simple. "In religion class, Mrs. Hatzenbeller said Jesus is the Bread of Life, Mom. Besides, He shouldn't be in the manger until Christmas."

Ever since Andrew put Jesus in the bread box, it has become a family tradition. Now, from the first day of Advent until Christmas Eve, Jesus sits on top of or in the bread box to remind us that He is the Bread of Life. Each time I reach for the bread, I'm reminded to say a quick prayer of thanksgiving for our daily blessings, including our daily bread. On Christmas Eve, almost ceremoniously, Andrew places the baby in the manger between Mary and Joseph.

After the Epiphany, we put the manger scene away for the year. All except for Baby Jesus; He goes back in the bread box as a daily reminder that just like our daily bread, the spirit of Christmas is an everyday, yearlong event.

Chapter Three

Party Time!
Participate in Life's Celebrations

Ye shall hallow the fiftieth year . . .
it shall be a jubilee. . . .
LEVITICUS 25:10 (KJV)

Life is full of high points and that is when Patricia Lorenz declares, "Party time!" Time to revel in joy and do a little jig. And, most importantly, it gives us occasion to thank God for all of our blessings.

From a jubilee celebration with seventy friends to a wedding in New York City, from celebrating Singles Day to meeting "Homerun King" Hank Aaron, from the ringing of Christmas bells to the Rose Bowl, Pat recalls plenty of moments filled with happiness and love. So put on your party duds and your dancin' shoes. It's "Party Time!"

A Jubilee Celebration

When my daughter Julia turned twenty-eight in 1999, she whined about her age. "I can't believe I'm this old!" she said wistfully. "I think I'm going to start counting backward. I'm telling everyone I'm twenty-six. In two years I'll be twenty-four."

I started thinking about the fact that Jeanne, my oldest daughter, would be thirty years old three weeks later. Then I started feeling old. How could I have a thirty-year-old daughter? Where did the years go?

Not long after that, I received a printed invitation to my friend Alice's jubilee celebration. On January 30, 1999, she celebrated her forty-ninth birthday, which to Alice meant that she was gloriously stepping into her fiftieth year . . . her jubilee year. She invited more than a hundred women friends to a hall for dinner and a program. More than seventy of us were able to attend.

The room was decorated with brightly colored balloons and flowers everywhere. After dinner, Alice talked with grace and deep appreciation about the women who had been the most influential in her life. There were hugs, tears, laughter and prayers. Then she darkened the room and lit a candle, and as each woman in turn lit her candle from the candle of the woman next to her, we all mentioned one, two or three women who had been the most positive influential forces in our lives. Many mentioned their own mothers or favorite aunts. Others named famous women — poets, writers, politicians, Mother Teresa.

By the time we left Alice's jubilee celebration, we were so happy to be alive that I practically flew home on the tail of one of those brightly colored balloons. Alice had made us feel wise and cherished and, most of all, appreciative of the age we had each attained.

Personally, I can't wait until October 2005 when I turn sixty.

A Wedding, Pure and Simple

"Mom, Canyon and I have decided to get married . . . in three days!"

It was my oldest daughter Jeanne, an artist living in New York City. She and Canyon had known each other for years, and our entire family rated him a ten on the scale of great catches. But getting married in three days?

"We were going to elope, but decided we wanted some of our friends there. We want you to come."

I began to stammer, thinking of my role as mother of the bride.

Jeanne interrupted, "We're getting married at City Hall. Then we're going to Riverside Park to have our own religious ceremony. We'll have a late lunch at an outdoor cafe, then take the Circle Line harbor lights cruise around lower Manhattan. All you have to do is get on a plane and join us."

The morning of the wedding, Canyon asked me to make a *chuppah*, a Jewish wedding canopy. Just give me an umbrella, a hot glue gun, lots of ribbon, and I'm in heaven! It was a grand chuppah.

I watched Jeanne get dressed in a lovely blue dress from the fifties that she had bought at a resale shop for fifteen dollars. An hour later, Jeanne, Canyon and I took the subway to City Hall where we giggled at the magistrate's forty-five-second civil ceremony. Later, in the park, Canyon and Jeanne exchanged rings again and read prayers in what seemed much more like a wedding than the courthouse event. It was a day of perfect weather and lighthearted wonder.

Best of all, it was a commitment before God and the state. A wedding, pure and simple, blessed with spontaneity, the laughter of friends, the deep love of husband and wife, and the awe and joy of one very proud mother, who learned that weddings come in all sizes, shapes and styles, and that if you just let it happen, the day will be graced with blessings.

'Tis Better to Give

"I hope people don't bring presents," my friend Diane moaned. "My basement is full of beautiful things I don't know what to do with as it is." Diane was getting remarried later in life, which meant trying to combine two households into one.

A gleam appeared in her eye. "What if we gave each guest a present, instead of the other way around?"

"I'll throw you a bridal shower," I said, catching her enthusiasm. "We'll wrap everything for you!" I sent out shower invitations requesting that the guests bring not gifts, but rather wrapping paper, ribbons, scissors and tape. The day of the shower, we gathered in Diane's basement. First she had us take gifts for ourselves, then we wrapped the rest of the items — picture frames, jewelry, glassware, trays, books, linens, silver and bric-a-brac. Every gift was tagged with a number. A corresponding number was put on each place card at the wedding reception.

The guests left the reception gushing over their gifts. After all, isn't that why you invite people to your wedding? To share in your joy.

Singles Day

According to the *Statistical Abstract of the United States*, there are 195.5 million adults in this country. Of these, 116.6 million are married, and 78.9 million have either never married or are divorced or widowed. Therefore 40.4 percent of all adults in this country are single.

My current period of singleness began in 1985. At first, I spent my single life waiting for the man of my dreams. But after a dozen or so years I decided the single life is a wonderful way to live. Instead of waiting for Mr. Right to come along, my other single friends showed me how to live my life with as much joy, gusto and fulfillment as married couples by concentrating on being a great friend to all sorts of people.

Since we have Mother's Day in May and Father's Day in June and Grandparents Day in September, perhaps we could have Singles Day in April. If I were in charge of Singles Day, I'd make greeting cards proclaiming the reasons why it's great to be single. Things like:

- You can sleep in the middle of the bed if you want.
- Toothpaste is always rolled up the way you like.
- The car seat is always in the right position.
- You can cook what you want when you want, including having popcorn for lunch or eating your dessert first.

- You can tear whatever you want out of the newspaper, even if you're the first person to read it.
- Your friends can drop into your home anytime without an invitation and nobody's going to get upset.
- No one is going to throw a fit if you put a little dent in the car.
- You can eat cookies in bed and listen to the radio at 3:00 a.m. without bothering anybody.

So to all you other single folks out there, Happy Singles Day!

Hammerin' Hank

I'm not an autograph collector, but in our home we do have one framed autograph. I got it for my youngest son Andrew in 1991 when I was working for a radio station in Milwaukee.

One day, baseball great Hank Aaron came to the station to promote his book *I Had a Hammer: The Hank Aaron Story*. During a commercial break, I asked Hank for his autograph. He smiled and wrote his name in big letters across a sheet from my radio station notepad.

Of course, Andrew was thrilled. After all,

Hank Aaron still holds Major League Baseball's record for the most home runs hit by any player. Though I'm not a die-hard baseball fan, I was even more thrilled than Andrew to have this man's autograph. Why? Because of the struggles Hank Aaron had during his career. He began playing at a time when few African American athletes even made it into the big leagues. And because of racism, he had to struggle against the odds time and again, often facing taunts and jeers from the world outside the baseball field.

Do you ever feel you're battling a war against all odds? Do pressures in your home or job make you feel you're not accomplishing anything worthwhile? Next time you feel that way, think about Hank Aaron. For more than twenty years he just "hammered" away, facing the struggles head-on, until he beat Babe Ruth's record by forty-one home runs!

The Great Indoors

I've lived in the Midwest most of my life and have learned to enjoy the four distinct seasons. The one month I've always found hard to live with, however, is November — a month of fickle, mostly dreary weather.

What I miss most in November is the sun. It's as if all these hazy gray November days are telling us, "Beware, Old Man Winter is going to get you and this is just the preview!"

If I could just appreciate November more! If I could just forget that I'm cold and all the beds have to be remade with thick woolen blankets, that all the big holidays are imminent and I lack energy to face them, and that icy rains will soon pound on my windows. . . .

So I decided one year, instead of moaning about November, to celebrate the great *indoors*. Here are some projects I planned:

- Make a pot of hearty soup and give jars of it away.
- Clean out one (that's enough!) closet.
- Read out loud to my grandchildren.
- Give a family member (or two) a long, soothing backrub.
- Have long, intimate talks over cocoa and cookies with my children and grandchildren.
- Call up some relatives I haven't talked to for years, just to say hello.
- Spend more time curled up with my Bible.

The more I thought about it, the more I looked forward to enjoying November!

Why don't you try it? You probably have special ideas of your own.

The Beautiful Sounds of Christmas

On Christmas Eve in medieval England, Scotland and Ireland, the village church bells tolled mournfully and slowly for an hour before midnight. It was the annual celebration of the devil's funeral. Then, just at the stroke of midnight, the bells rang out loudly, jubilantly, because it was believed that the devil died when Jesus was born.

Today, church bells and carillons across the land still call the faithful to church on Christmas Eve and morning, rejoicing that the Savior is born. The words "Merry Christmas! Merry Christmas!" are shouted, whispered and sung by friends, relatives, neighbors, co-workers, even strangers on the street.

This year, when the church bells toll, let's add to those beautiful sounds of Christmas a few beautiful sounds of our own:

"God bless you!"
"May I help you?"
"Thank you!"
"Praise God!"
"Welcome home!"

"I forgive you."

"I love you."

See how many beautiful sounds of Christmas you can say.

The Best Plan Is God's

For many years, when the University of Wisconsin Badgers football team wasn't doing so well, we still had our spectacular marching band. Everybody loved their wild and crazy "fifth quarter" presentation after each game. But in the fall of 1993 something wonderful happened. The Badgers had a 10-1-1 season and made it to the Rose Bowl for the first time in thirty-one years!

Armed with his recent "Most Valuable Percussionist" award, my son Michael and his fellow Badger band members were off to Pasadena, California. Oh, how I wanted to go to that game! I searched my savings and checking accounts, desperately trying to figure out a way to afford the airfare and hotel costs. I entered a newspaper contest where the prize was a trip to the game. I warned my out-of-state relatives who were planning to come to my home for New Year's weekend that I might be going to the game in person.

Well, none of it happened. I stayed

home, the relatives came (all thirteen of them!), and we watched Michael on TV as the camera focused in on him playing his duos and high-stepping his way through the most exciting day of his life. And we cheered, laughed, whooped and hollered as we watched the Badgers beat the UCLA Bruins in an upset.

I learned something that day. We humans don't always know what's best for us, but God does. I was much better off with my big family in my own home than I would have been in Pasadena fighting the crowd by myself. And I wouldn't have seen my son as clearly on his proudest day had I been there.

Groundhog Day vs. Candlemas Day

I'll admit it. I've never looked forward to or enjoyed Groundhog Day. No matter what the groundhog sees when he comes out of his hole, we Wisconsin realists already know that we're going to have at least six more weeks of winter. Probably more like twelve weeks of cold, dreary weather, if the truth be known.

Personally, I like the other holiday that falls on February 2 much better: Candlemas Day. Candlemas commemorates the presentation of the infant Jesus in the temple by Mary and Joseph. As Luke tells the story in his gospel, the old man Simeon, who has been waiting to see the deliverance of Israel, takes the baby in his arms and declares that He is the light of the nation's glory. Since the eleventh century, candles have been blessed on Candlemas Day in many churches to recall Simeon's words.

In northern Europe, where Candlemas Day is celebrated with gusto, tradition says that dark, snowy skies on February 2 offer hope of a quick end to winter, much like the Groundhog Day tradition in the United States. An old Scottish couplet proclaims:

If Candlemas is fair and clear,
There'll be two winters in the year.

But if that happens, at least we'll have the warm, bright light from those candles to give us hope for an early spring and warmer weather.

Today, in my home in Oak Creek, I'm going to light candles on the table at supper time. I'm going to think about how the light of Christ shines bright in our lives no matter what the forecast. I'll also dream about springtime and warmer temperatures, and perhaps even plan a few warm-weather vacations. I'll leave Groundhog Day to those folks around the country who truly do have a chance for less than six more weeks of winter.

George Washington

During a three-day visit to Philadelphia, I toured Congress Hall, Independence Hall and Carpenter's Hall — restored buildings that tell the secrets of where and how the Declaration of Independence was written and how our country began.

I felt a sense of awe as I gazed at the elaborate silver inkstand used to sign the Declaration of Independence more than two hundred years ago, and then ran my hand down the banister on the same stairway George Washington used in Independence Hall during most of his two terms as president from 1789 to 1797. From 1790 to 1800, the nation's capital was Philadelphia, while Washington, D.C. was being built.

What amazed me most about my trip through American history was Washington's humility. Our guide told us that the people of Philadelphia built an elaborate palace for Washington outside the city. Yet he refused to live in it, feeling his place was among the people. He also refused to serve more than two terms as president, even though he would have been easily reelected to a third term. Rather than follow the example of England's monarchs who ruled for their lifetime, Washington felt that no U.S. president should be in power more than eight years. In a precedent-setting act of humility, after just two terms, he stepped down and, in effect, handed the presidency to John Adams.

On Washington's birthday, February 22, what act of humility can we practice that could set a precedent for our families? Perhaps planning a vacation centered on the interests of other members of the family instead of our own. Or quietly doing things for them without any announcement. If we humble ourselves by being servants to those we love, perhaps we'll be revered in God's eyes the way Washington was revered by his countrymen.

A Mission to Do

I like celebrating St. Patrick's Day — I'm not sure if it's because I consider St. Patrick my patron saint (although there is a St. Patricia), or if I like celebrating the smidgen of Irish in my Scottish-Irish-English-French-German ancestry. It may be because I've always identified with St. Patrick as someone who had a mission to do and did it, in spite of great difficulties.

St. Patrick was actually born in Britain and sold into slavery in Ireland, where he turned to religion. After six years, he escaped back to Britain, but when he was twenty-two years old he returned to Ireland, determined to convert the Irish to Christianity. He eventually became a priest, then a bishop. In spite of great difficulties in life, he succeeded in making many converts, even among royal families.

St. Patrick is a great saint to identify with if you're going through hard times. I know when I was raising my four children, I was often lonely and fearful as I struggled to keep everything together. Like St. Patrick, I knew I had a tough job to do and that if I persevered and used my faith in God as a shield, I would be successful.

It wasn't easy, but St. Patrick taught me that the struggle itself is often the thing that makes us strong, gives us good character and makes us more interesting people.

The Gathering's What Counts

I like parties, and I especially like to have them in my home. As a single woman, I learned many years ago that in order to keep friendships alive, especially with my married couple friends, I needed to open my home and invite them in. But now that I'm in my fifties and an empty-nester, I don't particularly enjoy cooking, never bake and despise cleaning with a passion that would cause Mr. Clean's head to spin.

Doesn't sound like a recipe for a successful party, does it?

Years ago, when I inadvertently planned two parties for the same weekend, I learned how to pull off a good get-together without a fuss or a fume. One Saturday night I'd invited five couples over for dinner. On the invitations, I asked each couple to bring something from a different food category. All I had to do was set the table, prepare a simple casserole and make lemonade.

The next day I had a big party for all my single friends. The room was full of pot-luck snacks brought by everyone, thanks to my not being shy when they all asked, "What can I bring?"

Even though my cooking and cleaning genes have flown the coop now that my kids are grown, it's still very important for me to gather my friends at my house. And I certainly don't have to cook up a storm, bake fancy desserts or do a white-glove-inspection cleaning before they arrive. So far, nobody's noticed or said anything. What's truly important is the gathering.

Chapter Four

Pin the Tail on the Donkey
Make Light of
Embarrassing Moments

Work happily together.
Don't try to act big.
Don't try to get into the good graces of
important people,
but enjoy the company of ordinary folks.
And don't think you know it all!
ROMANS 12:16 (TLB)

No birthday party is complete without "Pin the Tail on the Donkey," the game where you're blindfolded, spun around and given the task to be right on target . . . yet usually miss. That happens in life, too, when we fall short of expectations — ours or someone else's — or when we embarrass ourselves or are not at our best.

Patricia Lorenz reveals those times when she held herself in too-high esteem, complained, butted into business other than her own, was bad-tempered, pessimistic and withholding. But eventually, always, she saw the error of her ways and tried to change for the better. She also learned to forgive herself and even laugh at her shortcomings. It's a gentle way of living, and she wants to let you in on that.

Humility, Humanness and Humor

Awhile back, I attended a celebration of the 125th anniversary of the Milwaukee Archdiocesan newspaper *The Catholic Herald*. At the reception, feeling somewhat cocky because I was one of the paper's regular columnists, I introduced myself to a number of guests. Then, as I nibbled on a piece of cheesecake, I studied the mementos and photos chronicling the newspaper's history that lined the office walls.

A tall, good-looking gentleman on my left was also looking at the display. Thinking perhaps he was one of the paper's staff and anxious to let him know that I was one of the columnists, I asked, "So what do you do here?"

He smiled and said with a twinkle, "I empty the wastebaskets."

When he turned to face me, I noticed his Roman collar. I laughed. "Oh sure, Father, and I bet you do a great job. What do you really do?"

Just then an acquaintance on my right said, "Your Excellency, I'd like you to meet Patricia Lorenz. Pat, this is Bishop Sklba."

I felt the color drain from my face, then immediately a whole new blood supply rushed upward. I was sure my cheeks were flashing neon red. "Oh, your Excellency, I'm I'm —"

Bishop Sklba interrupted with a hearty laugh as he put his arm around me. "Pat, it's my pleasure to meet you. And you know what? I really do empty the wastebaskets!"

I learned a good lesson that day. I

learned not to take myself or my position too seriously, and that a sense of humor and the ability to laugh at oneself are the mark of a truly great person.

A Disastrous Mistake

My daughter Jeanne, an artist, heard me bragging that I'd sold a story to an anthology that would have more than a million readers. A few weeks later, I had to admit that the publication decided not to use my piece after all. That's when Jeanne told me the following story.

In 1999, a well-known art curator in New York City commissioned four hundred artists, including Jeanne, each to make a painting that measured exactly two feet by two feet. He wanted to hang the four hundred square paintings in a perfect grid formation on three walls of a large gallery.

When Jeanne completed her watercolor, she had to cut it to the exact twenty-four-inch-square size. She went to an art store and purchased a surgeon's scalpel. Then, gingerly placing her steel ruler along the sides of the painting, she used the scalpel to slice through the heavy watercolor paper.

"Hey, this isn't so hard," she said, somewhat surprised at her dexterity.

She turned the painting twice and made two more cuts along the pencil line she'd drawn after carefully measuring out twenty-four inches on each side of the painting.

"Wow, I'm really good at this! I should be teaching other artists how to do it!"

She turned the painting to make the final cut. At the instant the scalpel left the paper, Jeanne realized she'd cut on the wrong side of the ruler, slicing off an inch and a half too much of her precious painting.

"Mom," she told me, "it was the minute I felt that cocky arrogance that I made the disastrous mistake!"

Jeanne salvaged the painting by applying adhesive to both pieces and attaching muslin to the back. But I'm sure some people who saw Jeanne's creation in that art show noticed the thin line where the painting had been cut and glued back.

I learned a lesson that day: Like Jeanne, I do my best when my focus isn't on myself but on the job at hand.

Stewing over Stamps

Years ago I tried buying stamps from a machine that accepted my fifty cents but did not produce any stamps. Later I wrote a terse complaint letter to the company listed on the front of the stamp machine, demanding that my fifty cents be returned as well as the twenty cents for the stamp on the letter I was writing.

Months later I still had not heard from the stamp machine company. Every time I saw that address tacked on my bulletin board I got angrier. I hated to be taken advantage of . . . even for a mere seventy cents.

Nearly a year after the incident, I was reorganizing my bulletin board. There it was, the address of that stamp machine company. The same mean, ugly feelings surfaced again. But this time I did something different: I said a little prayer, grabbed that paper, ripped it up and threw it in the wastebasket. With it went all the anger that had multiplied over the months.

Why had I kept that address for more than a year? Why had I wasted so much time being angry over a faulty machine and such a paltry sum? The minute I tore up the paper I was released from all that. Why? Because I had brought God into the picture.

The Adoption of Grandma Sarah

"It'll be great!" I said as much to myself as to my husband and four children. "Just like having a real grandma! We'll have her over for Sunday dinners. Introduce her to our friends. She never had any children of her own. Imagine how lonely she must be!"

As I finished tossing the salad for supper, my mind was on the Adopt-a-Grandparent program sponsored by our church. It sounded like such a marvelous idea for our family. Our children's grandparents lived far away in other states, and I felt we definitely needed a hometown grandma.

I could already smell spicy gingerbread cookies baking in her oven. I imagined sitting in her living room in an old cane rocker, listening to stories about her girlhood days.

Visions of turning her life around for the better danced before my eyes. I would fix a little extra food once or twice a week and provide her with some good home-cooked meals. And that knitted shawl that had belonged to my mother . . . wouldn't it be just the thing for our new grandma?

I told my husband, "Think of the advantages the children are going to receive! They'll learn to care about older people and to make time for them. They'll learn all about the olden days. Maybe she'll teach them how to bake those wonderful German pastries. The director told me her name is Sarah. She was born in Germany in 1890!"

"But, Pat . . ." my husband started to object.

"And she can teach the girls how to crochet. I'm sure she does that sort of thing. All grandmas do!"

The day finally arrived when we were to meet Grandma Sarah. She lived by herself in an apartment complex for the elderly.

The six of us — four children, my husband and I — all crowded into her tiny living room. Hats, coats, scarves and gloves were piled in a mountainous heap on one chair in her closet-sized kitchen.

I spoke first. "Sarah, we're so glad to have you for our grandmother. Would you like to come to our house for dinner next Sunday? And if you need to do any shopping, I'll be glad to take you this week." I was blubbering with enthusiasm, hoping it would rub off on the rest of my family.

Sarah pushed back a stray curl of white hair and tried to tuck it into the neat twist on top of her head. She spoke slowly, precisely. "My dear, I broke my hip last winter and I don't go out in the cold anymore. I'm afraid I might fall again. But I don't mind. It's not important to me to get out."

"Oh goodness." It was all I could mutter. "But what about church? Can't we at least take you to church with us?" I was determined to get her on our social calendar.

"No, not even that. Never missed a Sunday for nearly ninety years, but since last winter I don't even go to church anymore. Two nice folks from the visitation committee bring me communion every Sunday. So I don't mind not going. And I watch services on TV."

"Well then, we'll just have to figure out something else to do together. How about games? Do you play Monopoly or checkers? I noticed the lounge area down the hall with the game tables."

"My eyes, they just aren't what they used to be. Can't read the newspaper anymore. I listen to the radio a lot though. The big-print magazines are fine. But games? No. Just can't see well enough. I'm ninety-three, you know!"

Sarah was starting to get to me. The more enthusiastic I was about trying to make her life happier and more fulfilling, the more she seemed to cut me off at every pass.

"Well, we'll just visit you then and talk!" Out of the corner of my eye I saw my teenage daughter counting the tiles on the ceiling. My other daughter was fidgeting with the buttons on her sweater.

I continued, "The girls can come over after school some days. Maybe you can teach them to knit or crochet?"

Before Sarah could answer, I hurried on. "And Michael likes to walk to the shopping center next to your apartment with his best friend. They can stop in to see you every Saturday. You know how boys like cookies and milk from Grandma!"

Sarah pulled a bright orange, brown and gold afghan over her knees. She eyed Michael, who was writing his name on the steamy living room window with his finger. "Well, I do get lots of company. My sister comes every week. And my niece. I have the nicest niece. Reminds me of you, my dear. About your age, too. Five kids though. Her oldest just got married. Here, I'll show you the pictures."

At that moment, Andrew, our three-year-old, announced that he wanted a drink. He ran after Sarah, who was searching for the wedding pictures. Before I could grab him, he'd knocked a plant off the coffee table. My husband shot me one of those "It's time to get out of here" looks. I cleaned up the potted plant mess, then hustled the children into the kitchen for their coats.

"I'll come back to visit you this week, Sarah. Andrew's getting tired. That's why he's acting up."

"Well, I wouldn't know. Never had any children of my own. Just watched my nieces and nephews grow up from a distance. Haven't had any experience as a grandma. The church folks must have felt that I needed this program. Actually, I'm not a bit lonely. And I sure don't know a thing about being a grandma."

"You're doing great. It'll all work out," I muttered while I fiddled with Andrew's jacket. "Oh, I almost forgot. We brought you some presents. A canned ham, a candle and this shawl that belonged to my mother."

Sarah looked at the gifts and responded curtly. "My, what will I ever do with that much ham! It'll go to waste. I get Meals on Wheels. They bring my food every noon with plenty left over for supper. I'm not supposed to use my stove. Everyone's afraid I'll burn the place down, I guess."

She chuckled for the first time, then went on. "But you know, I don't miss it.

Baking, *schmaking*. Who needs all that work? Now I relax. You take the ham home. Your big family needs it. And the shawl, too. Dear, I have a drawer-full. And the candle. It's lovely, but please take it. I give away most of my things. Too much work dusting and cleaning everything. When you're ninety-three, you'll want life simple, too."

On the way home hot tears rolled down my cheeks. "How could she be so heartless! She wouldn't even accept our gifts!"

My husband touched my arm and said slowly, "Honey, you're expecting too much. She doesn't seem to be sad or lonely. And certainly not helpless. She's content with her life the way it is. Why should we clutter it up? You just can't rush in and start changing her life . . ."

"Changing her life? This grandparent program is a wonderful opportunity for her! She needs us!"

And later, musing about the situation, I recalled the verse in Leviticus that our church had used when they started the Adopt-a-Grandparent program. "Rise in the presence of the aged, show respect for the elderly" (Leviticus 19:32, NIV). Not only did Sarah need us, but it was my duty to show my respect for her as best I could.

Three days later, my spirits and optimism renewed, I popped in on Grandma Sarah. Six nuns, all dressed in short black dresses and veils, were also there to greet me.

Sarah explained. "My one sister, she's a nun you see, and these are her friends. They visit me every week."

I stopped over once again the next Saturday. This time I interrupted a visit by Sarah's niece and her son. They were just sitting down to an impromptu lunch of cold cuts and deli salads that her niece had brought.

Sarah was cordial enough. When she introduced me to her niece she said, "This is the lady whose family adopted me as their grandma. Imagine, me, a grandma!"

Sarah tried to find room for me at the tiny kitchen table. I told her that I'd already eaten and I'd wait in the living room. As I turned around she handed me a box of pictures. "Here, look at these. It's the Christmas party the landlord had for all of us here at the apartment," she said. "We have a party every month."

I settled into the overstuffed sofa, let the afghan fall around my shoulders and basked in the warmth of the room. I fumbled through the pictures. In every one,

Sarah was surrounded by laughing, happy people. I gazed at these pictures of happiness and listened to the bright chatter between Sarah and her niece.

Was this a sad, lonely old woman? Indeed not. My husband had been right all along. Sarah's life was already filled with love, with people, with small adventures and happy memories. Incredibly alert and healthy for her age, she was enjoying the last years of her life. What right did I have to interfere?

I had even been taking away some of her rights. She had a right to her privacy, a right to choose her own friends, a right to be alone when she wanted, a right to continue depending upon those she felt most comfortable with.

The verse from Leviticus came back to me: "Rise in the presence of the aged, show respect for the elderly."

Now I knew I wasn't showing Sarah respect at all. I was not respecting what she wanted. At last I began to understand that it was I who was in need. I had been willing to include her in some of my family activities with the hope of receiving so much more. I'd expected monumental gifts from Sarah . . . her precious time, her talents, the wisdom of her years, her influence upon my children and the tales of her past. I wanted her love, her devotion and her gratitude.

It was time to go. Gently, I refolded the afghan and placed it on the back of the sofa. I knew I'd never say good-bye to Sarah for good, but when I gave her a hug that day I knew it was the beginning of a much gentler, less frequent, less demanding relationship. Sarah had earned her peaceful, contented lifestyle, and I would never play havoc with that again.

Get Out of the Way

One morning I rolled out of bed at 6:30 to say a few cheery words to my sixteen-year-old daughter Jeanne, who was auditioning for the high-school musical that day.

I started my "Go get 'em, tiger!" cheer with, "Your hair sure looks nice, honey. I like it pulled up in a twist like that."

She grunted. "I hate it. It looks dorky — I'm going to take it down." (Does anybody know what *dorky* means?)

Undaunted, I proceeded. "Well, your singing sounds good. I'm sure you'll do fine at the audition today."

"I sound terrible. My voice stinks."

Determined, I went on. "Your new

sweater looks nice. I like that color on you."

"It's too big."

Well, if there's such a thing as getting up on the wrong side of the bed, Jeanne must have done it twice that day! And after striking out three times with her, I should have felt demoralized. But I didn't — something rose up in me, perhaps a good, strong mother's instinct. And with clear-sighted empathy I saw my daughter as an anxious young girl, nervous about an important audition. Silently, I prayed for her, and all day long I sent warm, confident thoughts her way.

Later that afternoon Jeanne waltzed in the door, hair still swept up in the becoming style, oversized sweater still swallowing her bones. "I got the part!" she said excitedly.

And after we hugged, she looked at me contritely and said, "And, Mom, I'm sorry I was so crabby this morning." I sighed with relief, and was reminded once more: Sometimes simply getting out of my child's way can be a way of showing love.

I'm Sorry

When my youngest son Andrew was eleven years old, he was talking on the phone one evening to his older sister Jeanne, an art student in California. I kept talking to him in the background. "Be sure to thank Jeanne for the hat she sent you." Then, "Find out what she'd like for her birthday." And, "Ask how her classes are."

Finally, Andrew said, "Mom keeps talking and interrupting me and I can't hear you, so I might as well hang up." He handed me the phone and went off to bed. It took me by surprise. I hadn't meant to ruin his phone conversation.

Half an hour later, I went to his bedroom. As I pulled the covers up to his chin, he opened his eyes. "I'm sorry, Mom," he said. "I didn't mean to hurt your feelings."

Andrew was saying "I'm sorry" to a mother who should have said it to him. As I apologized for interrupting his conversation, I realized that those were two words I hardly ever said. It was easy for me to say them only after Andrew had apologized.

The next time an incident called for it, I would be ready at the helm to take responsibility for apologizing. My teacher was a sensitive eleven-year-old boy.

Hurry-Hurry-Wait

Everything about my departure after my daughter Jeanne's whirlwind wedding in New York City seemed to be "hurry-hurry-wait." I hurried to pack, hurried down the three flights of stairs at Jeanne and Canyon's apartment, then I had to wait for the car service to pick me up. The driver hurried to the airport amidst horrendous traffic and honking horns, I dashed out of the car and hurried into La Guardia Airport, dragging my two suitcases, only to have to wait in line for check-in.

Then as I hurried to my gate, I rounded a corner and stopped cold. In the busy airport corridor were a dozen rocking chairs facing floor-to-ceiling windows that overlooked the runway. Several businessmen sat reading newspapers; another simply watched the activity outdoors. Two older women were chatting and rocking as if they were back home on the front porch.

How I wanted to plop my stressed-out, hurry-hurry body into one of those rocking chairs! But I still had to get through security, so I hurried there, only to have to wait fifteen minutes in line. At the gate, surrounded by stressed-out passengers, I waited another half-hour before we could board the plane.

Why didn't I sit down in a rocking chair and enjoy the view of the planes coming and going on the runway for ten or fifteen minutes? I wondered. *Why am I always in such a hurry?*

When I got back to Milwaukee, I started a new routine of sitting in the big yellow rocker on my deck with my morning tea and daily prayers. In the afternoons, I often find myself in my antique swing rocker in the living room, reading a few chapters of a good book or simply rocking and thinking. Now instead of "hurry-hurry-wait," my new motto is "rest-relax-rock."

Go Easy

My eight-year-old son Andrew and I went shopping for bright blue high-top canvas sneakers. There was only one other person in the shoe store with the salesclerk — a teenaged boy wearing loafers and no socks. He was paying for a pair of athletic shoes when we walked in. After he received his change, he walked over to the sport socks rack in the corner of the store.

The clerk went to the back room for a minute to find Andrew's size. I glanced up from my chair to see the boy shove a pair of fluffy white socks into his bag as he walked toward the front door. When the clerk returned, I whispered, "Did he buy a pair of socks?"

"No, why?"

"Well, I just saw him stuff a pair of socks into his bag." The clerk ran after the young shoplifter. As a firm believer in "tough love," I felt that if the boy got caught now, perhaps he would end his life of crime at an early age.

The clerk returned, smiling. "Those were Jason's own socks that he brought in to try on with his sneakers."

I had misjudged and wrongly accused the boy. It was then that I decided to concentrate on gathering all the facts before opening my mouth . . . especially when dealing with fragile teenaged egos. Maybe if I make a list of my own faults and look at it periodically, I won't be so quick to criticize others.

Michael's Mouth

My son Michael is thirty-two, funny and full of energy. Many years ago we moved from a small town in Illinois to the big city — Milwaukee. Michael and his two older sisters were pulled out of a small, cozy parochial school and placed in a large, bustling public school.

After a few months we heard reports from the two older girls that Michael had picked up some language on the playground that was a little rough around the edges. Michael and his dad and I had a heart-to-heart talk in the living room. Michael seemed impressed with the give-and-take discussion and promised to watch his mouth.

A few months later Michael's oldest sister came in from a rousing snowball fight with her pesky brother. "Michael's a garbage mouth! You should have heard what he said to me, Mom!"

Time for another heart-to-heart talk in the living room. This time a punishment seemed in order. After a lecture on the advantages of talking like a gentleman, one of which was being allowed to remain as a member of the family, Michael's dad said, "Michael, I think you should write a three-hundred-word essay on 'Why God gave me a mouth.'"

Have you ever seen an eight-year-old boy's face fall as far as his sneakers? That's the way Michael looked as he slumped off to his room to begin the torture of writing three hundred words.

What emerged on that paper a couple of hours later made up for all the teasing, horseplay and grumbling Michael had ever done in his young life — and for the street language, too. His essay is surely a prize-winning masterpiece, at least in the eyes of this mother. Here's part of it:

Why God Gave Us a Mouth

God gave us a mouth so we would be able to eat the fine food He gave us like fish, bread, and peanut butter and jelly on white bread. He also gave us a mouth so we would be able to blow bubbles for our baby brother or sister. And so we could sing in His beautiful house, the church. He also gave us a mouth so if we were working we could whistle and that would make us work faster because we wouldn't be so bored.

God gave us a mouth so we could smile and frown but mostly to smile. God gave us a mouth so dentists wouldn't go broke and lose their jobs! God gave us a mouth so we could say sorry when we get in a fight with some-body. God gave us a mouth so we could talk and reason with people before they really get us for it. God gave us a mouth so we could say, "I love my parents!"

Love, Michael

P.S. I'm sorry!

Michael's three-hundred-word punishment essay didn't quite capture the reason why we shouldn't use foul language, but it did express many of the reasons we can all be thankful God gave us a mind, a voice and a heart big enough to say, "I'm sorry." God also gave us a boy named Michael, and for this I'll be eternally grateful.

Simply and Clearly

I remember vividly one of the few times my second husband came to me for advice. As a high-school principal, he'd written a letter to send to the students' parents, and he asked me to comment on it. I read the entire two pages, then took a deep breath. As gently as I could, I explained that the sentences were too long and hard to understand, the words were too big, and the tone was too academic. Most of what he was trying to say was in the last two paragraphs — and those were very good.

I asked him to tell me what he was trying to say. It was wonderful, interesting, appropriate and poignant — and I simply wrote it down almost exactly the way he said it. The final version of the letter, shortened to less than one page, was something I'm sure the parents enjoyed reading.

All of us are sometimes guilty of "puffing up" our words on paper. A doctor once wrote on a chart, "Negative patient-care outcome." Why didn't he just write that the patient died?

Nowadays, whether I'm writing a letter to a friend, a work memo or a simple note to my children, I try not to impress others with my vocabulary and wordiness. Instead, I say what I want to say clearly and stop when I've said it.

Letter from Paul

It had been a terrible week. Both the washer and the dryer broke down. The clutch went out on the car. Then the mainspring on the garage door opener broke and I couldn't get the car out of the garage. Next, a half-dozen tiles popped up on the kitchen floor, which was in desperate need of replacement. My household repair budget was in shambles. Needless to say, the entire chain of events left me feeling bad-tempered and depressed.

Through all this, I had been missing my regular daily Bible reading, but now out of sheer desperation I started skimming through my Bible. I came to Ephesians and began casually reading. Suddenly, Paul was telling me what a great person I was! Then he started talking about how God understands me completely and how He showers me with His richness. Then he was practically gushing about how we are the gifts that God delights in! At the end of the fourth chapter he was telling me to "stop being mean, bad-tempered and angry." And toward the end of his letter he encouraged me to "pray all the time. Ask God for anything in line with the Holy Spirit's wishes."

When I saw that Paul had written his letter from prison, where he was put for serving the Lord, I decided that if he could be that optimistic in prison, I could certainly go about the business of trying hard to solve each household disaster one at a time. Eventually, everything was replaced or repaired. My smile returned, and I became a great fan of St. Paul's.

Are you feeling trapped by a person, situation or problem? Why not take fifteen minutes to read Paul's letter to the Ephesians? See if the shackles don't fall from your spirit and you find, instead, that you're infused with hope and love.

Pet Peeves

One night at a meeting of the SWILL gang (Southeastern Wisconsin Interesting Ladies League), we got on the subject of pet peeves.

Debbie said procrastination drove her crazy. "I hate it when I put something on my boss's desk ten days before it's due and then it sits there for two weeks before she even looks at it."

Jean said her pet peeve was people who misuse personal pronouns. "I hate it when they say, 'Me and him are going shopping' instead of 'My husband and I are going shopping.' "

Marjorie said her pet peeve was people who constantly crack their gum.

I said I disliked it when people make you take off your shoes before you enter their homes just so they can keep their carpets extra clean.

Sharon said people who grumble about everything really irritate her.

The next day I wondered what we'd accomplished by our round-table on pet peeves. Had we fallen into the category of people in Sharon's peeve? At the next meeting, to redeem myself, I suggested we each mention one human characteristic that we value the most.

Kay said, "I value a friend who has a

sense of humor even in down times because that shows joy and faith in God's love."

Sherry said, "I value people who can smile and reach out to people and make them feel welcome. I think a genuine smile really comes from God."

Jean, a clinical psychologist, said, "I think empathy, the capacity to be sensitive to the feelings and needs of others, is the most crucial human quality."

I felt much better after the SWILL gang left that night, knowing we'd given each other some positive goals. I, for one, am working on a genuine smile. And if I'm asked to take off my shoes when I enter someone's home, I'll flash my best grin, be more empathetic and enter joyfully.

Giving the Gift of Music

Every Saturday my mother drove me fifteen miles to the next town for my piano lesson. There were teachers in our town all right, but the *best* teacher was in the town fifteen miles away. So off we went, my mother and I, every single Saturday for six years.

The lessons took a big bite out of my parents' meager budget. And, of course, every Saturday afternoon of my mother's life was spent driving me to and from piano lessons.

I never did anything professionally with my music background. I never played accompaniments or entertained others. I simply confined the gift of six years of piano lessons to myself.

It's been more than forty-five years since I quit taking those lessons. I wonder if I didn't waste that gift by quitting before I entered high school or by begging off when friends asked me to play for them. I had simply taken the gift of six years of piano lessons, folded it up carefully and stuck it in my back pocket to be used only rarely "for me" when I felt like it.

Somewhere, could I find the courage to take my songbook to the nursing home and play for the residents? Why not this afternoon?

A Renewed Zest for Life

As my fifty-seventh birthday approached in 2002, I grew melancholy. When I looked in the mirror, I saw ten more pounds around my middle and lots more gray hair. My aching arthritic knee was a daily reminder that I was getting older.

Then I spent a few days with my eighty-three-year-old dad and my stepmom Bev in Illinois. Bev started bubbling about Dad's recent adventures. "Last month your dad rode in a race car at Chicagoland Speedway going one hundred and sixty miles an hour in a three-lap qualifying run." Bev's eyes twinkled. "The next week he did five take-offs and five landings in a small plane — twenty-nine years after the last time he piloted one." Then Bev reminded me that since he'd turned seventy-five, Dad had gone parasailing, ridden in a hot-air balloon and swooshed down an 1,100-foot alpine slide.

The next day I joined Dad and Bev at the Mendota Sweet Corn Festival. Dad loaded up the two 1930 American Austin cars that he'd restored in his seventies and early eighties. For the fourth year in a row, Dad won the trophy for having the best antique car in the parade.

The following day, Dad and I went for a bike ride along the canal. As we peddled faster and chatted about his next project, I suddenly felt young again. *I have great genes*, I thought.

I went back to Wisconsin with a renewed zest for life and plans to start a few new projects — including more bike rides.

Chapter Five

The Birthday Cake
Get the Most out of Life

The Lord God formed man
of the dust of the ground,
and breathed into his nostrils
the breath of life; and man
became a living soul.
GENESIS 2:7 (KJV)

The birthday cake is the pinnacle of a party. It symbolizes reaching a plateau and marking the moment with song and reverie. And it is here that Patricia Lorenz tells stories about how she gets the most out of life by recognizing certain truths about herself, her work, her family, her faith.

She fine-tunes her natural talents, taking a big pay cut but gaining joy. She learns different ways of praying creatively and spontaneously; she hears God's voice in the summertime breezes; and she sees that sometimes the only way to get through disaster is to get up, get going and persevere.

So help yourself to a slice of cake . . . or two . . . or three. . . .

That Little Dash

Gravestones usually have the person's name, date of birth, a little dash and then the date of death inscribed on them. Have you ever thought how much that little dash represents? Why, it's a whole life!

When I turned fifty, I figured my life was right at the middle of that little dash. Instead of being depressed about the Big

Five-O, I decided to enjoy the next fifty years with all the gusto, grit and flamboyance I could muster. That summer I snorkeled off the coast of Hawaii with two of my children. I stopped getting my hair permed and let it grow straight for the first time in decades. I made a solemn promise not to buy any clothes for three years. I simply wanted to stop shopping and spend more time doing more important, more exciting things, like traveling.

During my fifty-first summer I bought new in-line skates and made another solemn promise to exercise faithfully three to four times a week. Now that I'm fifty-eight, I'm ready for new adventures. Someday I'd like to work with Habitat for Humanity building houses. I want to hike the Appalachian Trail, take a photographic safari in Africa, study the New Testament with a real Bible scholar.

Remember, that precious little dash is all we have between life and death. Today, let's stretch our dreams and goals toward accomplishments that are bigger than ordinary.

Turn On the Music and Dance!

Just two months before my fifty-fifth birthday, I was feeling glum. It was the twenty-first anniversary of my mother's death from amyotrophic lateral sclerosis (Lou Gehrig's disease) when she was only fifty-seven. It bothered me that my mother started having symptoms of her disease when she was my age, especially since I'd been nursing a painful knee for nine months. However, X-rays and an MRI revealed a benign cyst, some minor tears of the cartilage, and a little bit of arthritis.

"Every fifty-year-old knee has a touch of arthritis," my doctor chuckled.

I breathed a sigh of relief, held my breath while the doctor gave my knee a shot of cortisone and went home feeling optimistic that I wouldn't have to have surgery.

That afternoon, to perk myself up even more, I went to an electronics store and bought my first CD player. Since I definitely needed to lose some weight, I figured that music might get me in the mood to do some regular exercise in the morning. I put the new CD player on the kitchen counter, bought some fast, upbeat music and devised my plan.

Each morning, as long as my knee felt

up to it, I'd go to the kitchen, turn on the music and dance for about forty-five minutes. I moved, stretched and hopped around the living room, feeling like a new woman. My energy level soared as high as my mood.

I'd not only dance around the living room, but through the dining room and right into the kitchen, where I'd come face-to-face with all the pictures of my loved ones on the refrigerator door. I prayed for them while I danced. And the more I danced, the more my heart sang out with the joy of life and healing and feeling good again, the better my knee felt, and the more prayers I said for the people on my refrigerator.

Don't Take Your Ducks to Eagle School

When I was a kid, I wanted to be four things when I grew up: a doctor, a trapeze artist, an airline pilot and a writer. But then I discovered that I have no natural talent in math or science. I've never balanced my checkbook and never got higher than a C in science.

Trapeze artist? Dad built me a stellar trapeze in our backyard, and I organized neighborhood circuses every summer. But in seventh grade, when I grew to five feet seven inches tall and faced the fact that I'd inherited my grandmother's large bones, I knew my torso would never fly from wire to wire on a high trapeze.

The airline pilot dream lasted through high school when I took flying lessons and discovered I'm not at all adept mechanically. I still have trouble remembering which dipstick is the oil and which is the transmission fluid when I open the hood on my car.

My fourth career choice held more promise. In second grade Mother gave me an old Smith Corona typewriter to play with, and I started writing with gusto. But by 1992, after writing more than forty thousand radio commercials, I asked myself, "Am I really happy doing this work?"

That's when a friend said to me, "Pat, don't take your ducks to eagle school. You can send your ducks to eagle boot camp, give them a little eagle hat, an eagle badge and an eagle T-shirt, but no matter how hard you try, those ducks will never become eagles. Maybe your real talent is something besides advertising writing."

I quit my job to stay home and write the kinds of things I wanted to write. I took a large pay cut, but my work, based on the real talent God gave me, suddenly became much easier and more joyful than anything I'd done before.

Makeup Prayers

It was early fall, and my morning prayer routine was starting to slip by the wayside. Sort of the way my personal appearance had slipped since I quit my job at the radio station to stay home and work.

Just before my forty-ninth birthday, my sister Catherine arrived for a weekend. She plopped a gift bag filled with eight little presents on my lap. "Happy birthday! Here's to a new you!" she said, her eyes twinkling.

I opened box after box. Lipstick, eyeliner, blush, eye shadows, little brushes to apply them all and a case to keep them in.

While I was thinking to myself that I like my "plain Jane" look, she whisked me into the bathroom and applied touches of highlighter, shadow and liner to my eyes. When Catherine finished my makeover, I couldn't believe my eyes. They looked bigger, brighter. Nice. I liked it all . . . the blush, the lipstick, the whole look.

"It takes a little time every morning, but if you do it every day it'll become a habit," she advised.

After Catherine's visit, I thought about my other "habit" that I'd let slip. Daily prayer. I thought, *What if I combined my prayer time with my makeup time?*

The next day, as I added a touch of eye shadow, I prayed, "Lord, please let these eyes of mine see the needs of others and respond accordingly." With the blush brush in hand I said, "Lord, my cheeks are pretty full. Help me to watch the fat grams today and exercise. Keep these cheeks smiling. Help me to see the good in others and to pass out smiles by the truckload."

Finally, the lipstick. "Lord, help me to use my mouth and the words that come out of it to Your glory. Help me to speak only with kindness."

My makeup routine is now a habit. So are my morning "makeup prayers."

Creative Prayers

I wrote radio commercials for a living. And after fifteen years, it was pretty hard to keep from repeating myself. One day I had to write ads for two different bottled water companies. Although both creative efforts sounded suspiciously alike, I turned them in.

At bedtime that night, ten-year-old Andrew and I were saying the Lord's Prayer as we have done every night since he was three. As usual, neither of us was paying close attention to the words we were saying. Somehow our recitation made me wonder if anyone would pay attention to the words of those bottled water commercials I'd written.

The next day I rewrote the commercials. I made myself think carefully about the benefits of good water. I wrote two new ads — one about the pleasures of drinking cold water in summer and the other emphasizing the purity of the water from the underground spring. The companies were pleased with my new ads, and I think that listeners really heard them.

The other thing I did was to start looking for creative ways Andrew and I could pray at bedtime. We began simply by making up our own spontaneous prayers. And on one night we read Psalm 27. We concentrated on the lines, "Don't be impatient. Wait for the Lord" (verse 14, TLB). Andrew had been talking for days about his lost Cleveland Indians baseball cap, and that night he asked God to help him find it. I knew Andrew had listened to the Psalm because he stopped talking about the lost cap after that. And some days later when he found it, he told me, "Look, I was patient and I waited . . . and found my cap."

Creative prayers. Begin your own search for fresh ways your family can converse with God and watch for new opportunities in answered prayers.

Satisfaction

After I quit my job at the radio station in 1992 to work at home full-time as a free-lance writer, a number of people suggested that I get a real job when times got tough financially for me.

"You should be a salesperson. You've got the personality for it. And think of the money you could make!" one friend suggested. "Why don't you consider teaching? Or at the very least, you could be a substitute teacher. They make good money," another offered.

All good suggestions, but I've learned that the paycheck isn't nearly as important as the satisfaction I get from doing my work and living my life. My daily commute is from my bedroom to my office downstairs. No traffic to fight. No stress. If I feel like going for a bike ride at eleven o'clock in the morning, I go. If a friend stops by for tea, I'm thrilled with the company, knowing I can catch up on my work later. If I feel like sitting on the deck for an hour in the middle of the day with a good book, I do it. If I want to spend an extra twenty minutes pondering a perplexing Proverb, nobody's there to insist I "get back to work."

I'll probably never make enough money to be called rich. But I hope to have had a happy, content and fulfilling life with plenty of time for the important stuff.

Tea, anyone?

How Much Is Enough?

At a conference for single people I attended a few years ago, a speaker told of a study that asked a large number of people who earned twenty thousand dollars a year if that was enough money. Eighty percent said no. Then the researchers asked people who earned forty thousand dollars if that was enough money. Again, eighty percent said no. Those who earned sixty thousand dollars a year were asked the same question. Eighty percent said, "No, it isn't enough." And so it went. No matter how much money people earned, at least eighty percent said it wasn't enough.

The speaker asked us, "How much

money is enough, do you think?"

My hand shot up. "I think the answer is ten thousand a year." I'd just sent in my income tax form for the previous year, in which my adjusted gross income was 8,673 dollars. Of course, my house is paid for and that income didn't include the Social Security I'd received for my son whose father died when he was nine years old. But nonetheless, my income was still below poverty level and I was blissfully happy in spite of the difficulty of making ends meet.

These days I'm often still in the poverty range because the Social Security ended in 1995 when Andrew was sixteen years old, but I don't mind a bit. I count my riches in glistening friendships, happy relationships with my children and family members, and the freedom to spend my life exactly the way I want. If a long walk in the morning with a friend or a leisurely bike ride in the afternoon is part of my day, I don't feel guilty that I'm not at my home computer. For me, those moments are more valuable than cash in the bank.

A Different Kind of Commute
Each morning after my cup of tea and a little breakfast I walk down one flight of steps,

through the family room, down a short hall into my office and, *zip-zap*, I'm at work. Total commuting time: twenty-one seconds.

My daughter Jeanne, a freelance artist in New York City, had a different kind of commute. Down forty-nine clanking steel warehouse steps where she lived in Brooklyn, walked two blocks to the bridge, climbed sixty-two steps to the sidewalk across the bridge, walked the quarter-mile across the bridge, down two flights of steps on the other side, walked three blocks, down two flights of stairs into the subway station, rode for ten minutes, got off, walked up one flight of stairs, got on another subway, rode for fifteen minutes, got off, walked two blocks in an underground tunnel, up one flight of stairs and emerged into the heart of midtown Manhattan. Then walked anywhere from a few blocks to more than a mile to wherever it was she was supposed to be that day.

After I made the commute with her for a few days during a visit, I watched Jeanne at work, painting scenery for an off-Broadway production one evening. She was positively radiant as she mixed paints and told me about the production. I learned by watching her create something beautiful that she absolutely loved what she does and that the commute was worth every step, every minute.

The joy Jeanne felt at work taught me that whether you get to work the hard way or the easy way doesn't matter. What matters is that you love what you're doing when you get there.

Ten Seconds Flat

Over the years during my career as a radio copywriter, I learned that anything said well can best be said with as few words as possible. I wrote thousands of radio commercials and learned early on that it's possible to say a lot in thirty seconds. Sometimes it takes fewer than ten. And many of those have become the most successful products and most memorable phrases in the listener's mind.

Remembering that one day, I decided to try an experiment. The next time I was angry with Andrew about leaving his room a mess, I tried using fewer words in my tirade. I cut down my usual "messy-room" raging from one minute to ten seconds flat. Andrew not only got the message quicker, he got the room cleaned faster.

"Mom, how do you like my room now?" he beamed to me at dinner after I had inspected his spotless headquarters.

I wanted to bombard him with my maternal wisdom about why he should keep his room clean. But I stopped short. *Remember your experiment,* I told myself. *Fewer words!* I looked at my son. "Andrew, you did great!" Neither of us had any hurt feelings for the rest of the evening.

It's true, I've got all the words in the world available to me, and I can go on and on and on if I choose. But why do it when less is more?

Look for the Light

I couldn't figure out what it was, but every November I used to lapse into a sort of depressed state — no energy, no ambition. I had to prod myself to do the simplest chores, and then only after I promised myself a nap. By January I'd gain ten pounds, nibbling out of boredom.

Then I read about Seasonal Affective Disorder or SAD, a form of depression resulting from a decrease in light during the fall and winter. Those affected by SAD slow down, oversleep, feel fatigued, crave carbohydrates, overeat, experience difficulties with work and relationships, and become pessimistic. The cause is a hormone in the brain called melatonin, which controls mood. Darkness produces more melatonin, causing depression, and light decreases it. Some people drastically affected by SAD move to the South where there is more light during the winter. Sitting under artificial light also helps certain people.

Now, every time those gray drizzly November days give me a case of SAD, I say to myself, *Look for the light, look for the light.* I make sure there are plenty of lights on where I'm working. I take walks whenever the sun is shining. On particularly gloomy days, I light a fire in the wood burner, turn on the lights, curl up with the Book of Psalms and fill my soul with the Light of God. You'd be surprised what twenty minutes of this can do.

Head of Household

Ask any separated, divorced or widowed person: When you're used to sharing your life with someone, to be suddenly single can be the most devastating, loneliest experience in the world. Starting a new relationship is the furthest thing from your mind.

When my husband and I divorced in 1985, I was so busy taking care of our four children and trying to carve out a career that I hardly had time to brush my hair, let alone think about meeting someone to spend time with.

But my children had different ideas. After a year of being my "dates" at movies, they began saying, "Mom, why don't you join that Single Again group at church and meet some men?"

I started praying wildly. *Help me, Lord. I don't know how to meet men or go out on a date. Besides, who wants a forty-year-old woman with four kids and a massive mortgage?*

But after another winter of being alone in the house every weekend while the kids were busy with their school friends, I worked up my nerve and joined the Single Again group.

A few weeks later the entire membership went out for a fish fry and dancing afterward. Twenty-one women and one man. And that poor guy danced with every one of us, bless his heart. When the dance was over, though, he left alone. Sort of limped out the door actually.

Lord, fish sticks in the oven at home would have been more fun.

For the next few months I kept my social calendar filled by attending my son's high-school basketball games, getting more involved at church and treating myself to an occasional dinner out with other single women friends.

Then one day it happened. I was invited out to dinner by a man I'd talked to on the phone at the radio station where I worked. I was terrified and my children knew it. "Mom, he's probably cute and maybe even rich! Maybe he'll take you to a really nice restaurant."

Well, he was rich all right. Too rich. And twenty years my senior. He not only took me to a very nice restaurant, but he also mentioned that he owned the place. He had just returned from South America and was anxious to take me to his penthouse to show me his antiques. And he celebrated every other topic of conversation with another drink.

I'm sorry about the lie, Lord. I really do like antiques.

At home that night, Jeanne, my oldest, was waiting up for me. "So, Mom, tell me all about him! Did you have fun?"

I took a deep breath. "Honey, I'm just going to lay it on the line. He was too old, too rich and he drank too much."

"Mother, with that attitude, you'll never find a man," Jeanne quipped.

She's probably right, Lord, but I'm just get-
ting used to being "head of household," and I'm
not sure it's time to complicate it. Besides, I
rather like the responsibility. Weren't You proud
of me, Lord, when I learned to use an ax to
split wood for the wood burner? When I revved
up the chain saw to cut the wood down to size,
I felt good. And, Lord, after a weekend of wood
splitting and sawing I don't have the energy to
smile politely, let alone look for a date!

A year later, after putting more than fifteen thousand miles on my little car, running the kids to their activities all over
kingdom come, it happened again. My
second date.

This gentleman was in advertising and
suggested I might do some copywriting for
him. We didn't talk business during
dinner; the conversation revolved around
his two passions in life: golf and tennis.
And for a woman who has never picked up
a club or a racket, it was a real "D & B"
night — dull and boring. Then when the
check came, he pointed out that the meal
was tax deductible. I didn't feel much like
a "date" after that.

When I reported to my kids, Jeanne replied, "That's what you said about your
date last year! You're too picky, Mom. Do
you like being single?"

So what's wrong with being single, Lord? Who am I anyway? Someone just searching for another half of a couple?

During the next year my social life seemed to get busier, without any more dates, I might add. I joined the religious education committee at church. I wrote for a local Christian singles magazine. Andrew, my youngest, and I made some new friends at a single parents and children's group that met for dinner and discussion every week. On Fridays we watched Michael play basketball and Julia cheerlead.

Although my life was filled with activity, I still wondered, "Who am I?"

The next year my friend Jody called. "You have to meet Ben. He's single, your age, no kids and wants to meet someone who likes quiet evenings watching TV. He doesn't go out much, but he's very good about fixing things around the house. You might like him."

Like him because he's a handyman?

Ben came over one Saturday afternoon, and I could tell right away he wasn't for me. Rather than waste any more of his time, I told him I had to run some errands. He said, "I'll come with you, and then we'll rent a movie to watch later on."

I sputtered a bit, then muttered, "Well, if

143

that's what you really want to do."

That evening, just as the movie began, my children started coming home — Julia from her baby-sitting job, Andrew from visiting his dad and Michael from his job at a local pharmacy.

So there we were in the family room. Me in my big green rocker next to the wood burner; Ben on the couch next to my chair; Andrew next to Ben; Julia next to Andrew; Michael on the love seat. A few minutes later Tony and John, Michael's best friends, came over and squeezed in on the couch and love seat.

Well, now, wasn't this cozy? Mom, her date, eight-year-old Andrew and four teen-agers. Michael kept looking at me sort of funny, like, "Where did you find this one, Mom?" I felt like I was on trial. Ben stood up, rubbed his slicked-back hair and went over to investigate the innards of the wood burner again. He liked that contraption, obviously more than he liked being in a room with jovial teens, a hip-and-trendy second-grader and a woman who yawned a lot.

Oh, Lord, I know my friends and I have been grumbling for three years about my "meeting a nice man," but I can hardly wait until this one goes home!

Such thoughts kept flitting through my head during the entire nine hours Ben stayed at our house that Saturday. When he finally left at midnight, I had to admit that being with someone for the wrong reasons is a lot worse than not being with anyone at all.

All right, Lord, I know. I'm not ready to find a nice man and settle down again. I'm already settled! And I like who I am. I feel as if there's a light that's all mine, burning inside me, reminding me who I really am. Just as St. Luke said: "If you are filled with light within, with no dark corners, then your face will be radiant too, as though a floodlight is beamed upon you" (Luke 11:36, TLB).

Yes, Lord, I know what that light is. And thanks to that special light that poked its warmth and brightness into the dark, cobwebbed corners of my heart, I know who I am at last — a capable woman, a caring mom and, most especially, Your loving Pat.

Letters to God

Have you ever been mad at God? I have, a number of times.

The first time was when I found myself in an abusive marriage with three small children and an alcoholic husband. The second time was during the months I had to watch my mother face death at age fifty-seven. The third time was when my second husband died when our son Andrew was only nine years old. Each tragedy caused me to be mad at God, at least temporarily.

Then I remembered something my mother did during the months before she died: She wrote letters to God. One said simply, "God, I have faith that You will help me out of this miserable time. How, I don't know. It's up to You. I love You, God."

I decided to give Mother's way a try, so during the times when I was experiencing bad things, I put my feelings on paper in letters to the Almighty. The act of writing it all down somehow relieved much of the anguish I was feeling, and before long it felt as if I were writing to an old friend who really understood what was in my heart.

These days, whenever my empty nest feels too empty or I start to worry about how I'm going to pay the house taxes that always come due at the end of the year or something goes wrong with my little red car, I write a letter to God. Instead of being mad at Him for the bad things that happen in life, I've learned to go to Him for comfort. And in time, somehow, all those letters are answered.

Don't Think About It

"This is your fourth pair of shoes in six months, Andrew!" I said. Andrew's feet had stretched out again, this time into a size thirteen shoe.

On the basketball court, at almost six feet and one hundred twenty-five pounds, Andrew looked like a skinny pole on water skis. More often than not, his long flat feet got in the way of a well-executed play. "I'm terrible, Mom! I can't even get up to the basket to make a shot!"

I knew how he felt. For two and a half years I'd had a wonderful friendship with Wayne, a widower. Now he said he wanted more, a commitment and marriage. There were no bells and whistles for me when it came to Wayne, just good friendship. And like the way Andrew's feet kept getting in his way, I knew my friendship with Wayne was getting in the way of letting him move on with his life to find the woman he would eventually marry.

The next few months, I floundered, alone and lonely every weekend, like an ungraceful fish out of water — the way Andrew felt on the basketball court. But then I heard Andrew's coach tell him not to think about his awkwardness. He taught him to concentrate on his lay-up skills instead. I decided to stop thinking about my loneliness and to concentrate on making new friends in the neighborhood. I also took on some extra work projects, switched to a church closer to my home and spent more time socializing with my married friends. Andrew and I both grew that year.

Old Glory

Like many "proud to be an American" citizens, I have always had the utmost respect for and devotion to the American flag. Old Glory flew on the front porch of my childhood home in Rock Falls, Illinois, on every holiday and on top of my dad's pontoon boat that cruised the Rock River for many years.

In my own home I have a sturdy nylon three-by-five-foot American flag that I fly proudly near my front door on every holiday and on days when I just feel like hollering from the rooftop that it's great to be an American, like the days when my grandchildren were born, or the day my friend won a cruise and invited me to go along.

My son Michael attended the University of Wisconsin, a school known as "the Berkeley of the Midwest," where students often find something to protest. In January 1991, during the Gulf War, a group of students decided to march down one of the campus's main streets. At one point, they stopped and set an American flag on fire.

Michael heard the commotion from his dorm room and followed the crowd to the burning flag. As a proud member of the National Guard Band, an organization he joined at age seventeen to help pay his way through college, he quickly pushed his way to the center of the crowd where the flag was burning and stomped it out. The protesters were furious, jeering and shouting insults.

Finally, the police arrived, and Michael was quickly whisked away in a squad car. "For your own protection, son," one officer explained as Michael was driven back to his dorm by a couple of officers who were no doubt proud that the young college student had defended the flag.

Here's to all the red-white-and-blue days in our lives. May Old Glory remind us to cherish our American citizenship every day, not just on patriotic holidays.

Highway Adventures

When my youngest child Andrew was seventeen years old, he wanted to buy a used motorcycle from our friend Pat McCardle, a police captain. I agreed only because Pat said he'd help Andrew keep the thing running and teach him about motorcycle safety. I figured the male bonding over grease and grime would be worth the price of my fear for Andrew's safety. And, of course, Andrew promised he'd wear a helmet every time he rode the cycle.

The first thing Andrew wanted to do when he got his license was take a trip across Wisconsin to visit his older brother Michael, who lived three hours away. He wanted me to drive the car just ahead of him, so I could carry his clothes and provide visual and moral support for his first great adventure.

Before we got out of Oak Creek, Andrew was stopped by a police officer because his headlight wasn't working. An hour and a half later, after getting the light replaced, we started again. An hour after that we stopped for lunch, and it started raining. I begged Andrew to leave the cycle there, so he could ride in the car with me in safety. Andrew assured me he could handle a little rain.

Back on the road, the rain got worse and Andrew drove in a torrent for more than forty-five minutes. Then, half an hour after the rain stopped, he ran out of gas. He finally figured out how to switch to the reserve tank, which allowed us to get to a gas station in the next town.

When we arrived at Michael's place, six hours after we'd left home, I was exhausted. "Andrew," I said, taking a deep breath, "I think you're ready to tackle the highways of life. You did a great job."

These days, now that Andrew is a young man, I'm ready to set out on a few adventures of my own, and who cares if I run out of gas!

How to Get Over a Disaster

Milwaukee had so much rain one week that much of the city and surrounding suburbs became flooded. I drove home from work through riverlike streets to discover my carpeted basement family room was underwater.

Desperately I threw beach towels on the floor, and spent the next hour sopping and wringing, sopping and wringing. Finally I just sat down on the steps exhausted, defeated and alone.

It was then that I remembered a newspaper article I had read sometime before about a shoe factory in Belgium, Wisconsin, that had burned to the ground shortly after Christmas. The next morning the owner of the company made arrangements to use an empty school in the small town for temporary offices. By noon that day he had already conferred with an architect on plans for another factory on the site. Then, the same day, he made arrangements to keep his employees working at another of his plants in a nearby town.

How inspired I was by his quick, no-nonsense reaction. How to get over a disaster? His actions seemed to say the only way is to get up, get going, start doing, rebuild . . . and to stay with the job until it's finished!

I stood up, threw more beach towels on the mess at my feet, pulled the carpet outside for a good scrubbing, finished mopping the floor, and by the next day I felt my family room would survive the flood — and so would I!

With the Wind

After our long, gray, cold winters, summertime in Wisconsin is welcomed like a long-lost friend. Fresh breezes from Lake Michigan, just a mile from my house, temper the sunny eighty-degree days, creating perfect weather.

One glorious July day I sat on my deck just soaking in the sounds of summer. First I heard the roar of a jumbo jet that took off from Milwaukee's Mitchell Field two miles north of my house. Then the birds — melodic blue jays, twittering finches, cawing crows — all scarfed up vittles from my four bird feeders. Next I heard the man down the hill making sad, guttural, unintelligible sounds caused by the debilitating stroke he'd suffered the year before. Finally, the magnificent electronic carillon of the church down the block. Twice a day, at 1:00 p.m. and 6:00 p.m., four or five pieces — hymns, gospel songs, classical and seasonal music — carry with the wind across the fields and road to lift our spirits.

As I listened carefully to those four sounds, it seemed that the voice of God was giving me some powerful advice:

Stop complaining about airplane noise. It doesn't upset you when you're in a plane going to visit a loved one. Be patient now, and let these passengers enjoy their travel.

My birds are chirping happily because you feed them. Don't neglect them in the winter when the deck is covered with snow.

The man down the hill needs your patience and your help. A kind word to his wife and an offer to mow their yard would be a good idea.

Just because you're not a member of the church with the magnificent bells doesn't mean you shouldn't be neighborly. It's time you let them know how much you enjoy the music.

SWILL and FOSSILS

When my dad, brother, sister and I bought a small vacation condo in Florida in 2002, I met many of the residents in the community, mostly snowbirds from the North, at the complex's large outdoor swimming pool. I discovered that many of them define their lives by their children's and grandchildren's accomplishments, and that many of them are wrapped up in their aches and pains.

After my first visit to the condo, I went home to Wisconsin determined to grow older with gusto. I even mentioned it to my women's group, SWILL (the Southeastern Wisconsin Interesting Ladies League). "When we go around the room to discuss whatever is on our minds, let's try not to focus so much on our children, grandchildren or health problems," I suggested.

Rosemary, a delightful woman in her seventies, giggled. "You'd love my FOS-SILS group, Pat," she beamed. "FOSSILS stands for Friends over Seventy Seasoned in Life Society. Just like SWILL, our

FOSSILS group has no dues, agenda, committees, minutes, rules, food worries, dress code or bylaws. We just have stimulating discussions. And we've agreed to avoid talking about our spouses, children, grandchildren, aches, pains and doctors.

Rosemary said her FOSSILS discussions have included how the older generation can help stop child abuse; how World War II compares with the war on terrorism; and why we provide so many activities for children these days instead of letting them have time just to goof off and use their own imaginations to find creative play.

Thanks to Rosemary, as I get closer to my sixties, I'm inspired to keep finding new, interesting topics of conversation with my old tried-and-true friends up North, as well as my new, somewhat older ones in Florida.

The Little Things in Life

I received a letter from the medical director of a Texas health center asking me to answer the question, "What is the key to contentment, fulfillment or happiness in life?" Seems he was preparing a book that would contain the answers to that question from "leaders and personalities all across our nation."

Well, I knew I wasn't a leader, so feeling rather perky that he'd proclaimed me, a mom from Oak Creek, Wisconsin, a "personality" in his form letter, I set out to answer the doctor's great question.

First, I pontificated about how one of the main purposes of education should be to help us discover the unique talent God has given each of us. I continued, "Next, we need to find a career that utilizes our particular talent. When we work at something we're naturally good at, contentment, fulfillment and happiness automatically follow. For me, chocolate chip cookies and naps work well also."

I'm not sure I captured exactly what the good doctor had in mind for his book, but the more I thought about it, the more I decided my last sentence was the most important.

Then I thought about lots of other "little" things that make me happy: the giant willow tree outside my office window; a good steaming cup of Irish Breakfast tea; snorkling; the new bike path that starts a block from my house; my grandchildren's big hugs. All these "little" things and hundreds like them make me contented, fulfilled and happy.

Chapter Six

Say Cheese!
Treasure Special Memories

"I will not forget you."
ISAIAH 49:15 (TLB)

Snapshot memories are what make getting older sweeter. Patricia Lorenz recalls a day on the lake when she learned her dad was "one of the good guys." There's also the night her parents woke her up, so she could share a root beer float with them. And the Sisters of Loretto doing double-Dutch and Grandma Kobbeman zipping by in a go-cart prove that getting older doesn't stop you from having fun.

There are a lot of other special moments that will warm your heart and make you smile, so flip through the pages to all of the sweet memories that await you.

One of the Good Guys

The world is full of temptations to be dishonest: cheating on income tax returns, padding expense accounts, bringing office supplies home for personal use . . . the list goes on and on.

When I was seven years old, my dad promised to take me for my first boat ride on the last day of a weekend camping trip. The anticipation was almost more than I could stand and I woke Dad at 6:30 the morning of our departure. We watched the sun rise over the glassy Minnesota lake, then headed for the boat office to rent one of the canoes lined up on the shore. The sign on the office door said, OPEN 11:00 a.m. My heart sank to my shoes. Dreams of my first boat ride vanished into the early morning mist.

I looked up through tear-clouded eyes in time to see my father pull a dollar bill out of his wallet. Then he wrote a note. "7:30 a.m. One dollar for a one-hour boat ride. Hope this is enough." He signed his name and address, then slipped the note and the dollar under the window.

That dollar bill and Dad's note to the management is more vivid in my memory than the boat ride itself. It would have been easy for anyone to "borrow" one of the unchained boats that day. There wasn't a soul around for miles. But for more than fifty years I've been warmed from the inside out by the discovery that my father was indeed "one of the good guys," and by the lesson that honesty means being honest *all the time*, not just when someone else is watching.

A Legacy of Love

When a thief broke into my father's house and stole the jewelry that had been my mother's, I felt the grief of her death all over again. Not only was *she* gone, but now I wouldn't have her jewelry to pass on to my children. The theft preyed on my mind so much that I began hiding my own good jewelry in odd places. No one would steal *my* legacy for my children!

A few days later I overheard them talking about their grandmother. Jeanne recalled how Grandma, even though her hands were crippled from the terminal disease that took her life, had painstakingly taught her how to embroider. Julia remembered the long autumn walks she took with Grandma along the creek. She said Grandma always stopped to exclaim over every colorful leaf that Julia retrieved from the water's edge. Michael said Grandma was the only person who could make sweet rolls so good you could eat a hundred! Each tale a special memory — a *jewel*.

I saw then that I didn't need Mother's jewelry to keep her spirit alive! The children had already received the most important heirlooms from Mother — her gentleness, her willingness to make time for people, her quiet sense of humor, her patience, her care for others. . . . If I just tried to be more like her, I, too, could pass on a legacy of love.

Brown Cows with the Folks

One Saturday night, when I was about seven years old, I'd gone to bed at my usual time, 8:00 or 8:30. By 9:30, I was into a deep, sound sleep.

"Pat, wake up," Dad whispered as he shook my shoulder. "Are you awake? We want you to come out to the kitchen."

"*Huh?* Why, Daddy?"

"Your mom and I decided to have root beer floats, and we don't want you to miss out. Come on, honey. There's a big 'brown cow' out there for you."

I padded to the kitchen in my big, pink, fluffy slippers and plopped down next to Mom at the old wooden table. I watched Dad scoop the vanilla ice cream into the blue, brown and yellow mugs that had been in my mother's family when she was a girl. The foam from the root beer tickled my nose as I chatted with my folks about school and our family plans for the coming holiday season.

I never felt more loved than I did that night in the kitchen as I groggily slurped root beer and ice cream with my parents. Why? Because Mom and Dad wanted my company enough to wake me up so I could be there. That one simple act did more for my self-esteem than anything I can remember before or since.

The Sisters of Loretto

One evening after a stressful day, when I still had six things left on my to-do list, I collapsed in a big green chair in the family room and picked up the photo album I'd started in sixth grade. It brought back a flood of memories of the fourteen years I was taught by the Sisters of Loretto.

I remembered the nuns going for rides in my dad's airboat with their long black habits tied down to keep them out of the propeller. In the winter, Dad bolted water skis on the bottom of the airboat and took them out on the frozen Rock River. Bundled up, the nuns rode sleds, saucers and toboggans behind the boat, screaming with delight. Once, when a freak storm left the entire school playground covered with smooth ice, the sisters let us bring our skates to school and extended our normal recess time so we could skate.

I remembered the sisters holding the

ends of our long jump ropes so we could do double-Dutch, or letting us beat them in dodge ball. Of course, they also had us read books, write stories, learn science, and memorize our times tables and the Baltimore Catechism. But it was the fun we had with those nuns that stayed with me. They must have had dozens of things on their to-do lists, but they knew how to relax.

I closed the photo album, determined to take a page from their book. Now, for at least an hour every day, I take an adult recess: I bike or walk along the shore of Lake Michigan, enjoy my favorite hobby of painting jars, treat myself to the $1.99 breakfast special at my favorite restaurant, read a book for pleasure, or simply take sidewalk chalk and draw flowers on the driveway.

Go-Cart Grandma

Every summer when I was a child, Grandma Kobbeman presided over our annual family reunion at Sinissippi Park in northern Illinois surrounded by her five children, their spouses and her twenty-four grandchildren.

One year, when Grandma was well into her seventies, she decided to ride her grandson's motorized go-cart. We held our breath when she squeezed into the seat, pressed the accelerator to the floor with her heavy brown oxfords and threw the little engine into World Cup competition. She flew across the track and down into the baseball field, barely missing the popcorn stand. As she headed for a row of poplars at the edge of Rock River, she released her foot from the accelerator and came to an abrupt halt at the edge of the water.

For a woman who had watched our country change from horse-and-buggy to men-on-the-moon, Grandma had adapted with a remarkable sense of adventure.

I later asked Grandma, "Why aren't you afraid to try new things?"

She just smiled and said, "Faith in the Lord is all you need, honey."

I'll always be grateful for Grandma's example — and the faith that never fails to inspire me when I feel afraid or am filled with doubt. That faith has inspired me to soar down a steep water slide with my children, ride on top of an elephant and take my first helicopter ride.

Isn't there something you've always wanted to try but were afraid to do? Do what Grandma Kobbeman did. Depend on your faith in the Lord and plop down on that go-cart!

Make-Believe

"Mommy, let's walk to the park," four-year-old Andrew begged that first warm day after a long Wisconsin winter. I wasn't really up for it, but Andrew persuaded me to abandon chores in favor of Mother Nature. He scampered out the door — and I ran after him.

"Let's climb that hill!" he squealed.

I stalled. "There are too many tall weeds."

"There's a path!"

At the top, he turned to run down. Before I could caution him to slow down, he'd fallen face down, then rolled the length of the hill. I expected tears and loud wails.

"Hey, Jill! I went up to get a pail of water, and I fell down and broke my crown!" His laughter was contagious.

The path led into the woods. Andrew stopped cold. "Gretel, I think we're lost. Did you bring any bread crumbs to drop on the path? What if the wicked witch gets us?"

"Oh, Hansel, the birds ate all the bread crumbs," I said. "You'll have to take care of that witch if we meet her."

We came to the footbridge that spanned the creek. Andrew scampered down the bank underneath the bridge. "Mommy, walk across the bridge."

I obeyed, wondering what he was up to now. Then a wee voice trying to sound mean and ornery shouted, "Who's that tramping on my bridge?"

I followed my cue. "It's just the littlest billy goat gruff. Don't eat me up!"

Walking home, the late afternoon shadows were taller than we were. Andrew put his small hand in mine and said out loud, "I love you, Mommy!"

Today, why don't you create some magic with a young friend and discover God's beautiful world?

Leaving Routines

The big yellow school bus swallowed up Andrew as I dashed for the front stoop to wave vigorously, blow him a kiss, then end the routine with more wild waving as the bus ground forward.

"Why do you do that silly waving routine every morning, Mom?" asked fifteen-year-old Julia.

"Every single day since Andrew started kindergarten last year, he has left the house with the words, 'Wave to me when the bus comes . . . and don't forget the kiss part.' "

"You didn't wave to me every day when I was in first grade," reminded fourteen-year-old Michael.

"That's because you had your two older sisters with you. Andrew needs to know he's not alone when he leaves. One of these days he'll get on the bus and forget even to look for me. But for now, I *like* feeling needed."

You know what? After that conversation, Julia started giving me a quick kiss on the cheek as she bounded out the door for the bus and Michael made sure to holler, "Bye, Mom!" even if I was in the bathroom getting ready for work. I like the "leaving routines" our family has that tie us together with a string of love and caring.

I've read that it takes seven days to make a habit. This week, why not form a new good-morning/good-bye habit with the people you love?

A Bit of Pleasure

I'd been feeling like an overloaded circuit. As a single parent with four children and three part-time jobs, I had absolutely no time for myself.

One busy day I looked out our dining room window at the barn-sized willow tree with a thousand branches hanging to the ground, forming a dome, and impulsively I found myself inviting six-year-old Andrew to have lunch with me under it. We spread a blanket, ate, read stories and tree-gazed.

The next day while running errands with a car full of kids, I happened to see a family of woodchucks popping their heads up and down in a cabbage field. I stopped the car, and we all watched the antics of these little wild creatures. That little reprieve from our rush-rush routine brought out a flurry of comments, questions and later an encyclopedia session.

The kids learned about woodchucks, and I learned how important it is to take time from my busy days to enjoy the little things in life. That picnic under the willow tree and the furry creatures in the field eased the stress and worry in my life.

Today, why don't you find something small, maybe even incidental, in your life and just plain enjoy it. You might be surprised to find that a little bit of pleasure can help dispel a mountain of troubles.

Outdoor Family Fun

I bought a used computer for my youngest son Andrew the summer before he started high school. Before long, that machine was a source of contention between us.

"Two hours a day on the computer is enough," I told him. He would have been happier with twelve.

When I reminded Andrew that there was too much life outside the front door to spend the summer cooped up in the computer room, he thought for a minute and asked, "Mom, what did you do for fun in the summertime when you were a kid?"

I told him about the airboat my dad built and how we skimmed the backwaters of Rock River in northern Illinois, looking for carp. I explained how one summer I'd organized a whole neighborhood full of kids and we'd put on a circus in our backyard and given the money to charity. I told him about the time my mother and I lay on our bellies in the grass twenty feet away from a gopher's hole, waiting to see it pop its head up, which it did.

My list of summertime activities made Andrew laugh. It also made me remember how my folks had worked to help us create outdoor family fun. That week I started planning special things for Andrew and me to do that summer. We designed and created a new flower bed, took a trip to Wisconsin's Kettle Moraine to check out the scenery, rummaged through a huge used bookstore in downtown Milwaukee, drove to a nearby college town to explore the campus, took bike rides. And one day I even took him out to a country road and gave him his first driving lesson.

It takes time, effort and organizational skills to plan family events. But the memories you give your children will last a lifetime.

One Sunrise Moment

October 12 is the official day for Columbus Day. It's also my birthday. And it was the day in 1987 when my youngest son Andrew, who was seven at the time, and I arose in the wee hours, drove the two miles from our home to Lake Michigan and waited to see something Andrew had never seen before — a sunrise.

At 6:30 a.m., we arrived at the deserted lakefront with our jug of hot cocoa and spread a blanket in the sand. Andrew and I snuggled close in the forty-degree weather as the cold lake wind slapped our faces.

We waited, shivered, snuggled closer, talked, sipped our cocoa and watched the clouds change color over the massive expanse of icy blue water. In the dusky haze of almost-light, I felt a sense of melancholy at being another year older. More light escaped over the thick clouds lying flat against the horizon. We talked about how flat the world looked from here. No wonder the early explorers were confused.

Suddenly, at 7:01 a.m., we both saw it. An incredibly bright concentrated speck of orange light. In seconds, the speck became an arc the size of a crescent moon and hopped up on the horizon like the top of a neon pumpkin. Andrew jumped up and started dancing in the sand. "Mommy! We did it! We did it! We saw the sun rise!" Throwing up his arms in victory as if he himself caused this incredible event, he flashed a grin as wide as a jack-o-lantern's and asked me to take his picture.

Suddenly, I felt a sense of timelessness. My birthday dreariness disappeared. Instead, I felt a kinship with Christopher Columbus who, five hundred years before, must have felt the same elation as he watched land appear on the horizon just ahead. That one sunrise moment promised the chance for a better life, an opportunity to start over.

One Glorious Moment

It was the first football game of the year, a nonconference match-up between our University of Wisconsin Rose Bowl/Big Ten champions and Western Michigan, and I was driving my thirteen-year-old Badger-red car to Madison from Milwaukee on a scorching August day. All the windows were rolled down because the air-conditioning was broken, and the noise on the interstate was deafening.

Threading my way through traffic jams, I finally found a place to park two miles away from the stadium and had to take a bus to the game, where I waited forty-five minutes for my daughter Julia and her husband to meet me. My already bad mood plummeted when I discovered that our seats in the fifth row at the forty-yard line were horrible because the visiting team was standing right in front of us, blocking our view of the field.

Suddenly, the 350-member University of Wisconsin Marching Band high-stepped onto the field to the roar of the crowd. And then the grand moment: My son Michael, who had just been given a full-time contract as the assistant band director, stepped up the eight-foot ladder and led the band in "The Star-Spangled Banner."

At that moment, I wasn't hot, thirsty or crabby about the bad seats. All the drum lessons and the band performances I'd attended for twenty years came to one glorious moment — my son directing the marching band at a Big Ten football game in front of seventy thousand fans.

As I wiped the sweat from my brow and the tears from my eyes, I was reminded of the sacrifices we parents make for our kids and, most importantly, how they can wipe out that debt in a single moment. Whether it's when they receive a diploma, get their first job, give birth to a first grandchild or direct "The Star-Spangled Banner" on a sweltering day, parental love has the ability to wipe out all the struggles, past and present.

Andrew Gets His License

When my son was preparing for his driver's test, I knew I had to convince him that driving on the busy, eight-lane interstate system of Milwaukee was different from navigating the two-lane streets in Oak Creek, Wisconsin. One day on the interstate, I got a brainstorm.

"Andrew, time me for one minute while I say aloud every single thing I'm thinking. Here goes.

"I'm looking in my rearview mirror, glancing at my side mirror. The guy in front of me is slowing down, the man in front of him has his blinker on to change lanes. I look in the rearview mirror again. The semi behind me is swerving into the left lane as we go around the curve and he's picking up speed. I look in my rearview mirror again and in the side mirror to my right. An older car is speeding up behind me in the far right lane with five teens in it. They pull into the middle lane behind me, in front of the semi, trying to pass me. I maintain my speed, giving them a chance to pass on the left. I glance into the rearview mirror. A police car's speeding up in the left lane. The speeders pass me. I see an open spot in the far right lane and signal to enter that lane just as the police lights go on behind the speeders."

I paused for a breath.

"Mom, that was only forty-two seconds."

"Well, do you get my point? So much is happening out here every single second, and you have to be aware of all of it!"

A few weeks later, Andrew got his license. In the meantime I started paying closer attention, not just while driving, but to everything around me. While riding my bike on the county's new bike trail, I memorized every scene: How the trail winds back and forth as if the designer was an artist. The wild-flowers growing in bunches as large as living rooms. The *clank, clank, thump, thump* of the new two-by-fours on the footbridge. . . .

First Date

"Mom, you realize this is my first real date?"

"What about the homecoming dance last year? That was a date."

"That was awful . . . formal clothes, parents gawking, taking pictures, slow dancing. . . . It wasn't like going out and really having fun. It was . . . well, anyway, this is a date."

"But you don't know these boys. [At least it was going to be a double date with Jeanne's best girlfriend going along.] They could be drug addicts or juvenile delinquents. They could be from broken homes. [Before those words even left my mouth I winced. I was a single parent, for heaven's sake!] Where do they go to school?"

"We met them at the forensics meet. They both go to the specialty school for the college-bound, downtown. Mother, they take calculus!"

A week later the doorbell rang. In walked Jeanne's girlfriend Amy with the two dates. One was a youthful clone of Ward Cleaver of *Leave It to Beaver* fame, a nice-looking boy in a brown plaid sport shirt and gray-rimmed glasses. He looked as if he loved calculus.

The other one — oh my gosh, the other one (*Please, God, don't let him be Jeanne's date!*) — was a cross between Son of Dracula and a beautician's bad dream. His name was Peter. He was dressed in black. ("He always wears black, Mom. It's okay, it's cool.") A black leather vest over a black shirt and pants, black fingerless gloves (I'm sorry, I don't get it . . . fingerless gloves?), black sunglasses (including the lenses) and black shoes.

Oh, thank goodness Jeanne's father isn't here to see this. Lord, please, help me say the right things. And again, *Lord, please don't let this one be Jeanne's date!*

My eyes became riveted to Peter's hair, which looked as if it had been dyed red, then cut with a lawn mower and moussed with machinery grease so it stood up in uneven spikes before being colored with thick black shoe polish. Vincent Price would have loved this look; I was appalled.

But it was the earring that finished off

his ensemble with an exclamation point. *Could that be a pop-tab from a soda can he's wearing?* I wondered as I clutched the arms of my grandmother's antique swivel rocker.

Soon we were well past the first formalities and I was trying my hardest to ask the kinds of questions fathers always ask their daughters' dates. I'd just finished the ones about if he had a job and was he planning to go to college — "Yes, ma'am," on both answers — when I steered politely into my question about his earring.

"No, it's an orchid. Silver. Would you like to see it?"

Before I had a chance to answer, Peter was hovering over my chair, proudly dangling his orchid earring (still attached to his ear) in my face.

"That's lovely," I whispered, wishing immediately that I hadn't used the word *lovely*. It wasn't a man's word, and I wanted to assure myself and the Black Maria standing before me that I wasn't doubting his masculinity in the least. After all, I'd just read an article in the newspaper that said anyone who was offended by men wearing earrings was just not "with it" because men in record numbers, real men, were wearing them as a matter of pride and principle.

Heaven help us. *Oh, Lord, whatever happened to V-neck sweaters, short brown wavy hair and penny loafers? What do I do, Lord? Can I actually send a daughter, who is still tied tightly to my apron strings, out into the night with a creature from the Black Lagoon? Lord, are You there?*

When I couldn't think of any more questions to ask either boy, I walked the four teens to the front door. Actually I was praying wildly to myself. *Please, Lord, send a tornado, anything . . . just don't let my daughter leave the house. I don't know yet what his dad does for a living, whether the family goes to church, if he likes children and animals, if he's . . .*

At the front door I expected to see a Harley-Davidson with a double-width sidecar sitting in the driveway. My racing pulse relaxed a little when I saw the older-model station wagon. Jeanne settled into the front seat. Now I prayed that Brown Plaid Sport Shirt would get behind the wheel. He didn't. Black Bandit did.

Where are my heart pills? I wondered. Then I remembered: I don't take heart pills.

When Amy and her date (how did they figure out who was with whom in such a split second?) climbed in the back seat,

Amy let out a scream. I hopped off the front step, expecting to see — heaven knows what I expected to see! When I reached the car, Mr. Plaid Shirt in the back seat was handing each girl a long-stemmed yellow rose and a peanut-butter-and-jelly sandwich on white bread carefully tucked into a plastic sandwich bag.

While the girls were *ooh*ing and *aah*ing, Mr. No Fingers in His Gloves turned around to me and smiled a banana-sized grin. "Peanut-butter-and-jelly sandwiches are a symbol of friendship," he said sincerely.

"Oh . . . my goodness," I stammered. Suddenly I couldn't think of one reason not to like this young man, earring and all.

"Be home at eleven-thirty," I said, smiling.

"No problem, ma'am. We have to be home at midnight and we live at least a half-hour away. We'll have the girls home before eleven-thirty."

And they did. And I shouldn't have worried about Jeanne's "first real date." When they brought her home at 11:15, both boys walked her to the door. And when they said good-bye, she gave each of them a quick hug. (She told me later.)

I've decided there's something about today's teens that has my generation beat hands down. They're expressive. They're individuals. They aren't afraid to be different. But then I've always been a sucker for peanut butter and jelly myself. And you know, that earring really was gorgeous.

Thanks, Lord, for loosening up the apron strings.

One Good Wing and a Prayer

Have you ever experienced a fear of flying? When I fly, I sometimes feel a little nervous during those first thirty seconds of takeoff. But then I remember an experience my dad had during World War II, and I suddenly become calm and thankful that I'm in a huge modern jet.

Imagine flying alone in a tiny, single-engine P-39 over the South Pacific during wartime in 1943. Suddenly, you see enemy planes just ahead and below you. A military intelligence magazine wrote about my dad's experience: "Lieutenant Kobbeman closed to one hundred fifty yards before opening fire. The tracers hit the enemy plane, but the Japanese pilot bailed out at ten thousand feet."

Then, from above and to the left, Dad's plane was hit by the enemy. "One was a direct hit in the tail section, which knocked off half the rudder and half the elevator. The left side of the horizontal stabilizer was also damaged. One shell hit the left wing, blowing out the landing light. Six shells struck the right wing. One hit the gas bay nearest the fuselage. Shrapnel entered the cockpit — injuring Lieutenant Kobbeman in the right foot and cutting the oxygen tube. Three 20-millimeter shells exploded inside the wing and blew a hole two feet in diameter. One shell hit the door of the cockpit, and the radio was shot out by shells and shrapnel. Lieutenant Kobbeman dived into clouds below and lost the enemy plane. Despite all this damage he was able to land safely."

"Weren't you terrified flying that tiny damaged plane over the ocean?" I asked Dad after I read the account. He said he just remembers flying one mile after another, knowing God was his copilot, and that one good wing and a very lengthy prayer got him back to land safely.

If prayer can do that for a young pilot whose plane is barely limping along over the ocean with enemy planes circling around, think what it can do for us on a day-to-day basis, whether we're flying a jumbo jet or driving a car to work.

Nudgings and Invitations

Christmas looked bleak. I had just become a newly single parent and was facing life alone. For the first time ever, one of my children wouldn't be with me on Christmas. Jeanne, my oldest, was a foreign-exchange student in Yugoslavia. Then the annual New Year's Eve get-together in Illinois with my relatives, to which I had been looking forward, had been canceled. And it was my turn to host the huge neighborhood Christmas party.

But here's what happened. On Christmas Eve, my other three children all wanted to attend the traditional family service at our church. Later, they insisted upon another family tradition: reading the Christmas story from the Bible before we opened presents. At midnight, my friends Bob and Betsy whisked me off to the candlelight service at their church. Two days later, they offered to co-host the neighborhood party, and all the neighbors pitched in to help with the refreshments. Then on New Year's weekend, my out-of-town family came to my home, ending the holiday week with loads of laughter and love. Because I gave in to the gentle nudgings and invitations of family and friends, that Christmas week became a memory I treasure.

Sometimes it's hard to get through the

Christmas season when you're alone. But if you stay open to letting others reach out to you, you may be surprised what happens during Christmas week.

God bless you . . . and know that someone in Oak Creek, Wisconsin, wishes you a very Merry Christmas.

Thank-You Letter Month

For thirty-two years Dad was a rural mail carrier, traversing fifty miles in his little VW bug to deliver mail to five hundred families. Every Christmas at least a hundred of those families gave Dad a gift in appreciation of his services. I loved all those homemade cookies, fudge, divinity and chocolate-covered cherries stacked up in our kitchen. Dad's cupboards overflowed with neckties, cuff links and bottles of aftershave.

Every January when the Christmas rush was over, Dad, who always said he hated to write letters, sat down at the dining room table and wrote a hundred or more thank-you letters by hand. More than 3,200 during his career!

As a child, I often joined Dad at the table in front of the fireplace and labored over my own thank-you letters. It became a tradition. A night of writing with my father . . . asking each other how to spell words . . . nibbling leftover mail-route peanut brittle. . . . But most of all, learning the meaning of the word *gratitude*.

Today, in my own home, January is still "thank-you letter month." My family and I write thank-you letters for every gift we receive from friends and relatives. But added to that tradition, we also write simple letters of appreciation to people who have meant so much to us throughout the year: the friendly clerk at the supermarket; the faithful postman who carries mail through sleet, rain and yapping dogs; the neighbor who watches my house when I'm away.

Gratitude. It's something we can never give enough of.

The 23rd Channel

I rarely watch TV in the summer, but during the long, cold winter months I'll flip it on and find myself sitting there for three or four hours a night. Then one Sunday, just before Lent, the following appeared in our church bulletin:

The 23rd Channel
The TV is my shepherd,
I shall not want.

It makes me lie down on the sofa.
It leads me away from the faith.
It destroys my soul.
It leads me in the path of sex and
    violence for the sponsor's sake.
Yea, though I walk in the shadow of
    Christian responsibilities, there will be
    no interruption for the TV is with
    me.
Its cable and remote control, they
    comfort me.
It prepares a commercial for me in the
    presence of my worldliness.
It anoints my head with humanism and
    consumerism, my coveting runneth
    over.
Surely, laziness and ignorance shall
    follow me all the days of my life,
and I shall dwell in the house watching
    TV forever.

After a long conversation with my son
Andrew, we agreed to give up TV during
Lent. He pouted the first couple of nights,
but then pulled out a board game on night
three and beat me in Chinese checkers for
the first time ever.

During the remainder of Lent, we read,
wrote letters, cleaned shelves, worked on
his science project and baked cookies. We

also took more time for bedtime prayers and bedside talks. I stopped saying, "I'll be up at ten, Andrew, when this movie is over."

It was the best Lent ever. This year, I can hardly wait for Ash Wednesday, now known as "TV Unplugging Day."

Beautiful Child

My fiftieth year was a blockbuster. I went to Europe for the first time in my life, chaperoning twenty-six teenagers! And that summer I even water-skied behind my brother's speedboat on the Ohio River. But the most important thing that happened to me that year after I turned fifty was becoming a grandmother for the second time.

Hannah was born a month early with a head full of thick, shocking red hair. The first time I saw her she was still in the neonatal intensive care unit at the hospital, attached to all sorts of wires and monitors, and sleeping in a heated bassinet. Her back seemed only a few inches wide as she snuggled into my hand. Her skinny little arms were punctuated with perfectly formed fingers that squeezed my little finger.

Holding and rocking my dainty, darling redheaded granddaughter in that hospital brought on such feelings of joy that during my two-day visit I practically begged my son, Hannah's dad, to let me go in instead of him during the few minutes each hour that one of us was allowed in the intensive care unit. Most of the time Michael gave in and stood outside looking through the thick windows of the nursery while I rocked and cuddled my precious grandchild.

As Hannah and I snuggled, I knew without a doubt that no matter what adventures I have, where I go or what I accomplish in my next fifty years, absolutely *nothing* can come close to the intense feelings and joy of being a grandmother.

Chapter Seven

Presents

Receive Gifts of Love

They presented unto him gifts;
gold, and frankincense, and myrrh.
MATTHEW 2:11 (KJV)

Presents are the best part of a party! Who doesn't like gifts specially chosen just for them? The anticipation beforehand and the satisfaction afterward are a couple of the happiest feelings we can have.

Patricia Lorenz gives us stories of the countless presents she has received in her life. Some of the gifts are tangible objects, such as the old worn smock she and her mother playfully and lovingly exchanged over their lifetime together. Or the advertising jingles that a co-worker rewrote to remind Pat of God's goodness. Some of the presents are acts of kindness that got her through one son's wedding, another son's illness and a speaking engagement. And a few of the gifts are those of faith shared and gratitude given.

Read on, and unwrap your presents today.

The Smock

It had long sleeves, four extra-large pockets and snapped up the front — a jaunty yellow smock.

I found it in 1963, during the time I was

a college student in St. Louis. I was home on Christmas break, pleased to be back with my family in Illinois and away from dorm life. Part of the fun of every vacation at home was the chance to go through Mom's hoard of rummage, destined for the less fortunate. She regularly scoured the house for clothes, bedding and housewares to give away.

Looking through this odd collection one day, I came across the yellow smock. Just the thing, I said to myself, to wear over my clothes during art class next semester.

"What? You're not taking that old thing, are you?" Mother said when she saw me packing it. "I wore that when I was pregnant with your brother in 1954!"

"It's perfect for art class, Mom. Thanks!" I quickly slipped it away in my suitcase before she could object.

The smock became a part of my college wardrobe. I loved it. All during college, it stayed with me, always handy and comfortable to throw over my clothes during any messy project. Even though the underarm seams had to be reinforced once or twice, plenty of wear remained.

After graduation I moved to Denver and wore the smock the day I moved into my new apartment. I wore it on Saturday mornings when I cleaned. Those large pockets made a super place to carry dust-cloths, wax and polish.

The next year I married. When I became pregnant with my first child, I sought out the old smock and wore it during those big-belly days. Though I missed sharing my first pregnancy with my family because we were in Colorado and they were in Illinois, that smock helped to remind me of their warmth and protection. I smiled when I remembered that Mother had worn the smock when she was pregnant.

By 1969 the smock was at least fifteen years old. That Christmas I patched one elbow, washed and pressed it, wrapped it in holiday paper, and sent it to Mom. I tucked a note in the pocket saying, "I hope this fits. I'm sure the color will look great on you!" I hated to give up the smock, but I was prompted by something I'd read in Proverbs 11:24 (TLB): "It is possible to give away and become richer!" Little did I know how true that would be.

When Mom wrote to thank me for her "real" gifts, she mentioned that the yellow shirt was lovely. Mother never mentioned the smock again.

The next year my husband, daughter and I moved from Denver to St. Louis. On the way, we stopped at Mom and Dad's house in Illinois to pick up some furniture. Days later when we uncrated the kitchen table, I noticed something yellow taped to its bottom. The smock!

And so the pattern was set.

On our next visit home I secretly placed the smock between the mattress and the box spring of Mom and Dad's bed. I don't know how long it took her to find it, but more than a year passed before I got it back.

This time Mom got even with me. She put it underneath the base of our living room floor lamp, knowing that as a mother of three children, all under three-and-a-half, housecleaning and moving lamps were not everyday events. Sneaky!

When I finally found the smock, I wore it often while refinishing furniture. The walnut stains on its front added more character.

Unfortunately, our lives were full of stains, too. My marriage had been failing almost from the beginning. My husband and I were finally divorced in 1975. The three children and I prepared to leave our home in St. Louis and move back to Illinois to be closer to the emotional support of family and friends.

As I packed, a deep depression overtook me. I wondered if I could make it on my own with three small children to raise. I wondered if I would be able to find a job.

I paged through my Bible looking for comforting words. In Ephesians 6:13 (TLB) I read, "So use every piece of God's armor to resist the enemy whenever he attacks, and when it is all over, you will still be standing up."

I tried to picture myself wearing God's armor, but all I saw was me wearing the yellow smock. And why not? Wasn't my mother's love a piece of God's armor? I smiled and remembered the fun the smock had brought into my life. My courage was renewed. Now I could face my future.

Unpacking in our new home, I knew that it was my turn to get the smock back to Mother. The next time I visited her, I carefully tucked it under all her winter sweaters in her bottom dresser drawer, knowing sweater weather was months away.

Meanwhile my life moved splendidly. I found an interesting job at a radio station, and the children thrived in their new environment.

A year later during a window-washing energy spurt, I found the crumpled smock hidden in my ragbag. Something new had been added, however. Emblazoned across the top of the breast pocket were the newly embroidered words, *I Belong to Pat.*

It took me awhile, but I finally found the solution to the dilemma of how to make it "hers" once again. I gathered my embroidery materials and added an apostrophe *s* to *Pat* and the word *Mother* after that. Now the faded yellow smock proudly announced, *I Belong to Pat's Mother.*

Once again I zigzagged all the frayed seams. Then I enlisted the aid of a dear friend, Harold, to help me get it back to Mom.

This was my finest hour. Harold arranged to have a friend of his mail the smock to Mom from Arlington, Virginia. We enclosed a letter announcing that she was the recipient of an award for her good deeds. The gift award came from "The Institute for the Destitute."

On Easter Sunday the next year, Mother managed the coup de grâce. She walked into our home with regal poise, wearing the yellow smock over her Easter outfit as if it were an integral part of her wardrobe. I'm sure my mouth hung open, but I said nothing. During the Easter meal, a giant laugh choked my throat. But I was determined not to break the magical unspoken spell the smock had woven into our lives.

I was sure Mom would take off the smock and try to hide it somewhere in my home, but when she and Dad left, she walked out the door wearing *I Belong to Pat's Mother* like a coat of arms.

A year later, in June 1978, Harold and I were married. The day of our wedding we hid our car in a friend's locked garage to avoid the usual practical jokers. After the wedding, while my new husband drove us to our honeymoon suite in Wisconsin, I reached for a pillow so I could rest my head. The pillow felt lumpy. I unzipped the case and discovered a gift, wrapped in wedding paper. I thought perhaps it was a surprise from Harold. But he looked as stunned as I. To my complete shock, I found the yellow smock.

Mother knew I'd need that smock as a reminder that a sense of humor, spiced with love, is one of the most important ingredients for a happy marriage.

Inside one pocket I found a note. "Read John 14:27–29. I love you both. Mother." I quickly opened my Living Bible and found the verses:

I am leaving you with a gift — peace of mind and heart! And the peace I give isn't fragile like the peace the world gives. So don't be troubled or afraid. Remember what I told you — I am going away, but I will come back to you again. If you really love me, you will be very happy for me, for now I can go to the Father, who is greater than I am. I have told you these things before they happen so that when they do, you will believe in me.

The smock was Mother's final gift. She had known for three months before my wedding that she had a terminal disease, amyotrophic lateral sclerosis (Lou Gehrig's disease).

Mother died thirteen months later at age fifty-seven. I must admit that I was tempted to send the smock with her to her grave. But I'm glad I didn't because it is a vivid reminder of the love-filled game she and I played for more than sixteen years.

Giving to God

When my mother died in 1979, Dad gave me a box of papers from her desk. Included were her down-to-the-penny household statements for each month during my childhood years.

Every month she paid eleven bills by check: house payment, taxes, insurance, utilities, groceries, etc. The rest of the family income was placed in ten separate envelopes labeled *church, school expenses, clothes, gifts, repair and improvement, dues and licenses, doctor-dentist, Dad's allowance, Mom's allowance,* and *savings.*

The June 3, 1960, ledger states that she wrote $274 in checks. The cash in the envelopes totaled $130. Our family of five was living on $404 a month. In spite of the tight budget, Mother and Dad were giving more to the church than they were keeping for themselves. Mom kept $10. Dad kept $10 . . . and $24 went to the church.

Have I followed in my parents' footsteps? Hardly. The excuses come too easily. Four children to put through college. A big mortgage. An emergency that might come up. The vacation fund.

As a child, I never had the slightest notion that my parents inched their way through on such a tight budget. Yet every month they gave no thought to doing any less for the church than the absolute maximum that their tiny budget could stand. Maybe that's why I felt so rich as a kid.

God Is Like . . .

It was one of those months when Murphy's Law prevailed in my household. The TV and stereo both broke within two days of each other. Before I could take them to the repair shop, my computer died. Two of my children were sick, and when I tried to go for medicine the garage door broke. Then a friend called in tears to say her father had died unexpectedly.

"God, why? How can You dump so much on us at once?" I asked. I felt my faith wavering.

The next day a friend at the radio station where I was a copywriter dropped a piece of paper on my desk. It said:

God is like a Ford — He has a better idea.

God is like Coke — He's the real thing.

God is like Pan Am — He makes the going great.

God is like Alka-Seltzer — Try Him, you'll like Him.

God is like Bayer aspirin — He takes the pain away.

God is like Tide — He gets out the stains that others leave behind.

God is like Frosted Flakes — He's *grrreat!*

God is like Hallmark Cards — He cares enough to send the very best!

My friend's list changed my thinking and lifted my spirits. Soon I decided I could be a little more like Timex — Take a lickin' and keep on tickin'.

America's Melting Pot

During a trip to New York City years ago, I visited one of its famous museums. On a self-guided tour, I was thunderstruck by a massive painting covering an entire wall, the famous *Washington Crossing the Delaware*.

I stood in awe of the lifelike color, the feeling of movement, the sheer size of it. I studied the determined expressions on the faces of George Washington and his men as they pushed through the ice with wooden oars that cold Christmas night in 1776.

But what really struck me was the artist's name, Emanuel Gottlieb Leutze. Had a German painter created one of America's most treasured historical paintings? Later I learned that Leutze was born in Germany in 1816, immigrated to Philadelphia with his parents when he was nine years old, grew up and studied painting in his adopted homeland. At age thirty-five, he captured this piece of American history on canvas.

Would it surprise Washington to learn that a young German had created a quintessentially American treasure? Surely not. After all, hadn't Washington fought for American liberty with the assistance of fellow patriots with names like Lafayette and Pulaski, Von Steuben and Salomon? And didn't Washington value the melting pot quality that America had been founded upon?

When Washington led his men into battle, it was to fight for an America of richness and diversity and true freedom for all. Who better than Leutze to paint Washington's brave soldiers?

Ash Wednesday

Every Ash Wednesday when I was a child, all the teachers and children at our parochial school knelt at the altar in church to receive a cross of ashes on our foreheads. It was a sign of humility: "For dust thou art, and unto dust shalt thou return" (Genesis 3:19, KJV).

As an adult, I didn't attend Ash Wednesday services, mainly, I suppose, because I didn't want to "wear my faith on my sleeve" (or my forehead) in front of people all day. Having ashes on my forehead would force me to explain why they were there and what they meant, and to speak openly about my faith.

But one Ash Wednesday at the radio station where I worked, I spotted three or four people with ashes on their foreheads. Then I heard one of them explaining the tradition to another of our co-workers. "They're ashes, Mike. For Ash Wednesday. The cross symbolizes the life Christ gave us by His death on the cross. It's the beginning of Lent, a time to pray, fast, and think of ways to be less selfish and do more for others."

She made it sound so easy. The ashes on her forehead had given her an opportunity to do a little witness for the Lord without being the least bit pushy or pious.

Her example inspired me. On Ash Wednesday I will attend service and wear the cross of ashes on my forehead. And should someone ask me about them, I'll gladly share my faith with them.

Calling in the Troops

When my son Andrew was in eighth grade, he suddenly came out of the funk that had weighted him down after the death of his father four years earlier. During those years, he'd been wonderful at home, but at school had acted out and his grades were poor. Then, that first quarter in eighth grade, Andrew made the honor roll! I was thrilled, but Andrew was despondent.

"Mom, the kids all think I'm a nerd now that I'm making good grades. They liked me better when I was goofing off all the time. It's not worth it!"

I talked, pleaded, praised and coaxed my son, and I prayed earnestly, too, but it was as if he couldn't hear me. I learned a mother's words and love weren't enough. So I got busy. I made copies of Andrew's report card and a letter explaining the situation, and sent them to Andrew's big brother in college, to his grandfather in Illinois, to my Uncle Jim (a retired Air Force general who is one of Andrew's favorite people) in Omaha, Nebraska, and to my brother in Louisville, Kentucky. I called in the troops.

Every one of them called or wrote inspiring letters of encouragement to Andrew, and gradually I noticed that he stopped talking about hating school. His good grades continued. I was relieved — and I also found that I didn't have to do it all by myself.

Remember Single Moms

The most wonderful card I ever received was the handmade, beautifully painted Father's Day card my daughter Jeanne sent me for Father's Day a few years after I became a single parent. I'd been both mother and father to her, she wrote, and she just wanted me to know how much she appreciated it.

Jeanne's thoughtfulness made me think about Mother's Day, an event generally orchestrated by fathers. They take the kids shopping and help them buy gifts and flowers for Mom. Some husbands take their wives out for brunch to celebrate her special day. But when there's no dad around, a single mom is lucky if a thoughtful teacher has organized the making of a Mother's Day card during art class. Often there's nothing special about that day for her. I once spent the whole day alone.

I'd like to ask a couple of favors of you. First, think about all the single moms you know. Think about how Mother's Day is in some way the most important day of the year for them, because they aren't wives anymore — only mothers. And they usually do it while holding down full-time jobs and trying to make ends meet.

Second, ask if you can "borrow" the children of a single mom for a few hours before Mother's Day. Take them shopping for gifts — not expensive ones, but something she can unwrap excitedly on Mother's Day morning. Help the children wrap the gifts, if necessary. The children will be excited about the whole idea. But that mother — she'll appreciate it more than you can imagine.

Beach Glass Lesson

I collect antique hat pins, unusual napkin rings and beach glass. *Beach glass?*

Yes . . . right off the shores of Lake Michigan, just two miles from my home in Oak Creek, Wisconsin. I've gone collecting by myself, but mostly I'm with the children or a friend visiting from out of town who's anxious to see the lake. At the shoreline, I immediately start walking with my head down.

"What are you looking for?" one friend asked.

"Beach glass. Little bits of green, brown, clear, aqua, pink, blue and red glass, probably from old bottles that have been worn down smooth as pebbles by the waves. I sort them by colors and keep them in tall glass jars at home in a window."

"Oh, here's one!" she exclaimed.

"Nope, it's too sharp. Still needs a few years of waves lapping across it to smooth it out."

"Reminds me of my rough edges when I shout at the children," she said.

"Or me, when too many repair bills turn me into a raving maniac."

"Or when I'm cranky at work for no particular reason. Guess we all need to smooth out our rough spots. Think I'll take this rough piece of beach glass home with me as a reminder."

The Gift of Water

Water has always been a big part of my life. I grew up just a few blocks from Rock River in Rock Falls, Illinois. Since 1980, I've lived in Wisconsin, just a couple of miles from Lake Michigan, which is as beautiful as an ocean. My dream is to live someday on the very edge of a body of water. I don't care if it's the ocean, a river, lake or pond. I just want to be able to look at the water every day.

Strangely for such a water lover, I'd never been much of a water drinker, until the summer of 2000. My son Andrew had been hospitalized a couple of times the previous two years for dehydration during his bout with ulcerative colitis. I started nagging him to drink more water, and I decided I should heed my own words. So that summer I started drinking water with gusto.

My goal was sixty to one hundred ounces a day. I bought sixteen- and twenty-ounce water bottles and kept them filled and refilled in the refrigerator, and within a week of trying to start the new habit, I was doing it. Now I never leave the house in my car or on my bike or on in-line skates without a water bottle. And I drink it all day long inside the house. I'm addicted!

When I started drinking more water instead of those expensive sodas, juices, teas and lemonades, I started feeling better, lost some weight and had more energy than I'd had in years.

Water. What a simple yet marvelous gift the Lord has given us. It's the most basic ingredient for life, and if you have excellent water from your tap as we do in Oak Creek, it's practically free!

Wally and Shirley

The Monday before my son Michael's wedding, the reminder board in my front hall listed seventeen things that needed to be done that day to prepare for the rehearsal dinner for thirty at my house the following Friday and for the sixteen houseguests who would begin to arrive in three days. All I could do was shudder and ask God to send me a guardian angel to help me get everything done.

That morning, Wally and Shirley Winston pulled up in their RV. They were here to attend the wedding and spend a week in Wisconsin visiting old friends.

Shirley immediately saw the list on the board. "Well, let's get to work," she said. Wally gathered up brooms, the hose and fifteen-year-old Andrew, and headed for the backyard patio to get it ready for the rehearsal dinner. Shirley and I headed for the grocery store. Then we started cooking. She not only thought up fabulous entertainment and food ideas, she also organized and set out everything while I was at the wedding rehearsal. She and Wally even stayed up late cleaning after the dinner party.

The dinner and the whole wedding week were a great success, but I could never have pulled it off alone. Through Shirley, Wally and my reminder board, God showed me how important it is to make our needs known to others — and that guardian angels don't always have wings.

Breaking the Ice

It was a simple gesture that helped me overcome a big fear I had about public speaking. In a few weeks I would be speaking to my son Andrew's eighth-grade English class about my work as a writer for magazines and newspapers, and I was anxious. I'm a better writer than speaker, and wanting to make a good impression, I agonized over it.

Then one Saturday, I attended a church women's luncheon and found myself seated next to Ellen, the key speaker. "I'm much more comfortable with our meetings of twenty people," she whispered to me, "but today we are a group of one hundred. I'm terrified!"

As Ellen walked nervously to the stage, the program chairwoman who was about to introduce her suddenly stopped. Her face brightened and she said, "Before Ellen begins, you must see her shoes!" All eyes fell on Ellen's shoes. The group said *Ooh!* and *Aah!* and then applauded at the sight of her stunning black velvet flats embroidered with bright red, green and gold designs. Ellen blushed, then laughed and joined the applause. "Isn't she lovely to get us all into the spirit?" the chairwoman said. With that, the ice was broken, and Ellen delivered a talk that was both relaxed and inspired.

When I stood in front of Andrew's class weeks later to give my talk, I remembered the spontaneous gesture that preceded Ellen's speech. I didn't have to be all serious; my talk could be chatty. As I looked out at the class, my eyes met Andrew's. He was beaming. "Andrew," I called out, "why don't you tell your class why you wanted your mother to speak today?"

"Mom's great," Andrew said proudly. "And I think you could learn something from her." His classmates giggled and cheered. My talk went very well and, in fact, the children had more questions than there was time to answer. So I was asked to return on another day. And you know what? I did.

The *Buzz-Hum* of Faith

Buzz, buzz, buzz . . . hum, hum, hum. The sound could be the background for relaxation tapes. But this *buzz-hum* is the sound of three IV poles, lined up next to my eighteen-year-old son Andrew's hospital bed, pumping fluids into his arm. This young man is supposed to be careening through his last month of high school — writing that last essay for English class, bragging about how many hits he got in softball, getting the brakes fixed on his motorcycle. Instead, ulcerative colitis eats at his intestines.

For the first three days I'm calm and serene. I read something by Sam J. Ervin, Jr., that says faith is an inner spiritual strength that enables us to face the storms of life with hope and serenity . . . and I'm proud of my inner spiritual strength.

By the end of day four, my son is cranky. Four days without solid food, punctuated with pain and constant intrusions into his personal space, have left him with no social skills. He complains about everything, declares that he's sick of visitors and phone calls, and in the end he reduces me to tears. I'm not such a pillar of strength after all.

That night I whimper to Pastor Tom, "What's wrong with me? I'm losing it. Doesn't my faith guarantee serenity?"

"Nonsense," he says. "You need to get out of here. Take care of yourself for a while. I'll stay."

I leave, afraid that if I don't I'll burst into loud shaking sobs. I head for my friend Betsy's house, where we walk, talk and finish off the visit with cold drinks, brownies and hugs.

Back in my son's room, I settle into the chair next to the IV pumps. *Buzz, buzz, buzz . . . hum, hum, hum.* As I listen, I understand that faith flows like medicine through an IV, sure and steady. Sometimes it buzzes. Sometimes it hums. For now the humming lulls me to sleep.

Chapter Eight

Party Favors
Pass On Kindness

It is more blessed to give
than to receive.
ACTS 20:35 (KJV)

The little doodads that we get at parties are always fun. These playful items are that extra something to acknowledge the guests for their time, presence and gifts.

In "Party Favors," Patricia Lorenz recounts stories of kindness passed on from a few people to the entire community, from individuals to her, and from her to others. Read about fourth-graders who campaigned to feed the homeless, or how Pat's dad and his friend cleaned up the town's canal. Discover the importance each one of us holds in lessons learned from a broken-down typewriter, and behold the generous returns from a yard sale where everything is free!

Kazoos All Around!

When my children were small, the junk drawer in the kitchen was always loaded with kazoos. One time when Michael was a teenager and grousing about something or other, and his little brother Andrew was pouting because it was his bedtime, and the girls (also teenagers) were arguing about something or other, I opened the junk drawer and pulled out a handful of kazoos. I started playing and marching around the kitchen, adding to the cacophony at hand. Before long, the whole gang had kazoos in their mouths, making silly music with me. The laughter that followed erased the bad moods, and I've been a kazoo fan ever since.

Why don't you stop by a party-supply store and pick up enough kazoos for your entire family and a few extras for friends and relatives? When you're serving dessert tonight, place a kazoo on each person's plate and watch the fun begin.

Your children may think you've suddenly become one rung short of a ladder, one card short of a deck, one slice short of a loaf, one cent short of a dime . . . never mind, that's another game you can play with your kids.

Onx Kxy

Xvxn though this typxwritxr is an old modxl, it works vxry wxll, xx-cxpt for onx kxy. You'd think that with all thx othxr kxys working, onx kxy would hardly bx noticxd. But just onx kxy out of whack sxxms to ruin thx wholx xffort.

Havx you xvxr said to yoursxlf, "I'm only onx pxrson. No onx will noticx if I don't do my bxst." But it doxs makx a diffxrxncx, bxcausx to bx xffxctivx, a family, an organization or a businxss nxxds complxtx participation by xvxryonx to thx bxst of his or hxr ability.

So if you'rx having onx of thosx days whxn you think you just arxn't vxry important and you'rx txmptxd to slack off, rxmxmbxr this old typxwritxr. You arx a kxy pxrson, and whxn you don't do your bxst, nothing xlsx around you works out thx way it's supposxd to.

Doing for Others

The winter before my dad's sixty-ninth birthday, he and his retired friend Fritz decided to clear away trees and brush along a canal, just a few blocks from Dad's house. Every morning, Dad and Fritz bundled up and with their gas-powered chain saws blasted away the overgrowth on the slope next to the water. By springtime, they'd cleared a mile-long stretch six to eight feet wide. The next winter they did 1.2 miles, completing the project.

Impressed with the canal's new look, the Rock River Development Authority widened and resurfaced the path along the canal for bikers, walkers and joggers, and in July organized raft and canoe races. Then the Department of Conservation did some landscaping and added a ramp for the handicapped to the path.

Because of the initiative of two retirees in their late sixties, a beautiful new state parkway was created for the whole town to enjoy. And Dad says the harder he worked those two winters, the better he felt and the more energy he had. "Doing something positive for the town makes me feel good about myself!" he added.

Is there a project that might improve your town? Cleaning up debris along a river or creek? Planting flowers downtown? Painting old park benches? All it takes is one person to get the project started. Could it be you?

Fourth-Graders Take Action

When the fourth-grade religion class at St. Matthew's Church learned that food was being wasted at Milwaukee's sports arena, they went into action. Seems that a health regulation required that all food cooked or warmed (sausages, hot dogs, pizza) or food from packages that had been opened (deli sandwiches, buns, salads, pretzels) had to be thrown out at the end of the night. So the fourth-graders wrote letters asking if the leftover food could be given to the four shelters for the homeless located within blocks of the arena.

In less than two weeks, a response came from a lawyer saying that arrangements had been worked out with the health department so that the unused food could be given to people at the shelters after each sporting event.

What happens to the leftover food at the restaurants, sports arenas, movie houses and concession stands in your town? Could you be the one to find out and perhaps start the wheels in motion for getting that food to the hungry? Why not call your favorite restaurant and ask what is done with its leftover food each night? Could you be the one to pick it up and deliver it to a shelter for the homeless one night a week? Could you find half a dozen friends to help you?

A Good Deed

I once read about a woman who described herself as coming from an "intact single-parent family." I like that phrase. As a single parent of four, I don't want my children to think of themselves as "children of divorce" or products of a "broken" home. But the fact remains that with only one parent in the home, it's difficult time-wise and energy-wise to do it alone.

The U.S. Census Bureau estimated that one out of every four American children under eighteen lives with just one parent. If you're looking for a good deed to do right in your own neighborhood, why don't you find a single parent and offer some specific help?

Provide carpooling. Watch his children once a week, so he can volunteer at church, go to the library or shop by himself. Invite her to dinner some Saturday night when her children are visiting their dad. Stop over some evening for a cup of tea (single parents long for adult conversation in the evenings after the children are in bed). Offer to trade her mending or cooking skills for mowing her lawn or helping with household repairs. Tell them that they are doing a great job as single parents.

A New Kind of Garage Sale

I've probably hosted fifteen or more garage sales in the past twenty years. It's work, hard work: clean out the garage, set up tables, unpack the boxes of junk, price everything, make signs, post them, put an ad in the paper. Then comes the real work. By midday you're so hot, tired and cranky from arguing price with every customer who thinks haggling is a national pastime that you're ready to close up shop in favor of a cool bath.

Those days are over for me. One summer I discovered a new kind of garage sale. I simply went through my house and garage, threw everything I wanted to get rid of onto some tables set up out by the street, and made a huge sign that simply said, FREE.

Then I went to work in the house. Every so often I'd look out the front door to see if any of my junk collection was disappearing. By two o'clock, two-thirds of it was gone. By the end of the day, the only things left were one shoe that had no mate, two well-used purses and an old metal garbage can with a hole in the bottom.

I enjoyed that sale so much that I've done it every year since! And I will continue to do so until I pare down my fifty years' worth of collections to the point where I can move to a smaller home some day and not suffer shock when I try to cram a gallon's worth of stuff into a quart jar.

Just think, if everybody had "free sales,"

parents of older children could share the baby clothes and toddler toys with young couples who really need the stuff. Older couples could get rid of the items they've enjoyed for thirty years without a hassle. New home owners could have the rakes and lawn equipment not needed by those moving to condos.

What all do you have that you can give joyfully to others?

Without a Hitch

I could hardly believe it. All three of my older children were in college.

It was September 1990, and in one day I'd driven more than four hundred miles to get two of them settled in two different University of Wisconsin campuses. On the way home that night, I wondered how I'd fill up my time. *Will the kids need me anymore? Are my mothering days for my older children over? What will life be like with just Andrew and me rattling around the house?*

The next week I sent all three college kids a "Welcome to College" letter. I sent airline tickets to Jeanne in California, so she could fly home for three weeks at Christmas. I mailed Julia a box of snacks, along with a check to cover the tuition increase she hadn't counted on. Then I got a pleading phone call from Michael asking me to send him a batch of my homemade granola for late-night studying in the dorm. I lit the oven and started mixing the ingredients.

During the next few months, I wrote letters, visited them on campus and sent them goofy gifts. Doing those things made me feel so needed that I sailed through that first year of missing them without a hitch. I discovered that if a relationship is going to be alive and vibrant, it's up to me to keep it that way.

College Commandments

After thirty years of parenting, my nest was suddenly empty. In August 1998, I said good-bye to Andrew on the campus of Arizona State University. But even though my nest was empty, my mothering days weren't over by a long shot. Andrew still needed me. Not to send care packages with cookies, clean underwear and extra dollars stuffed inside a few magazines; no, he needed me to teach him the College Commandments:

I. *Thou Shalt Not Bring Thy Dirty Laundry Home to Mom.* Nothing ruins a perfectly good weekend visit more than the thought of five loads of your jeans and T-shirts languishing on the floor in the laundry room.

II. *Thou Shalt Not Call Thy Mother on the Phone Collect.* If I accept your collect calls, it doesn't teach you anything about fiscal responsibility.

III. *Thou Shalt Not Spend Money Frivolously.* Since your brother and sisters (and now you) got through college with grants, scholarships, loans, work-study programs and two to three part-time jobs each, in addition to the money I've saved for all of you, it seems that your education is the most important part of these four years, and not a car, expensive clothes or exotic trips during spring break.

IV. *Thou Shalt Have Thine Own Checking Account to Pay Thine Own Bills.* Checking account good; credit card bad. A checking account teaches you the value of having money in the coffer to pay for the item before you buy it.

There were days when I missed Andrew desperately. But there was one consolation. My daughter Julia said it best in a letter she wrote to me not long after Andrew started college. At the top she'd typed, "A parent is not a person to lean on, but a person to make leaning unnecessary."

The Good Book

I love to browse in libraries and bookstores. Depending on my mood, I can choose AD-VENTURE, HISTORY, SELF-IMPROVEMENT, TRAVEL, HEALTH, ROMANCE or MYS-TERY books, and read to my heart's content. It's also fun to share a really good book with a friend. Have you ever wondered why they call the Bible "the Good Book"? I think one reason is that it is filled from cover to cover with those seven categories.

Starting today and all week, let's find these seven special-interest categories in the Bible and read the Good Book each day from a different perspective.

Day 1: ADVENTURE. Read about Jonah. What could be more adventurous than being swallowed up by a great fish?

Day 2: HISTORY. The Bible is packed with history, especially family history, in I and II Samuel.

Day 3: SELF-IMPROVEMENT. A reading through of Proverbs can help you become new and improved!

Day 4: Travel. Try Acts . . . and make sure you have an atlas handy!

Day 5: Health. For advice on not drinking, read Jeremiah 35. For some great exercise tips, read I Timothy 4:7–10.

Day 6: Romance. The Song of Solomon is very romantic!

Day 7: Mystery. Read Revelation, and try decoding the meanings of the numbers and colors.

By the end of the week, you'll have a whole new appreciation of the variety of stories that are in the Bible. And since it is the Good Book, maybe you'd like to share your findings with a family member or friend each day.

Times Two

It wasn't always easy to find the time, but when my children were preschoolers I read aloud to them twice a day, before the afternoon naps and before bedtime. We went through hundreds of library books together. They all went to college, and I think reading helped get them there.

When Andrew, my youngest child, was in fourth and fifth grade, every time he had a science test I read the chapter to him the night before, adding my own comments here and there. He usually aced the tests, and we both learned a lot about science during those years.

You know, when you read aloud it's like reading twice, because two of you get the benefit. Why don't you try it? Tonight, you could:

- Offer to read a homework chapter aloud to your child or grandchild.
- Read an interesting article from today's newspaper to someone in the family.
- Read a chapter from the textbook to your spouse, so he or she can understand what it is you're studying.
- Read an article from a current magazine to Grandma, who may find it hard to read because of poor eyesight.
- Read aloud the entire Bible this year; start with one chapter a day!

Write It Down

I'm a great list-maker. The chalkboard near our front door is forever filled with lists of things to buy, errands to run or repairs to make. My children have also become list-makers.

Years ago, when my daughter Jeanne desperately wanted a pair of gerbils, she made this list of reasons why she should have them.

Having Gerbils Will . . .

1. Teach me to care for other living creatures.
2. Make me study longer alone in my room.
3. Help use the oxygen my plants are producing.
4. Keep Mom company when Andrew goes to kindergarten.

Jeanne's persuasive list not only earned her a pair of gerbils, but it reminded me that when we organize our thoughts by writing them down, it's much easier to accomplish our goals.

Starting today, why don't we write down our spiritual goals for the week and check them off as we accomplish them? How about these for starters?

1. Offer to help repair or cover the church hymnals.
2. Leave a note to a family member on the bathroom mirror praising a job well-done.
3. Compose a new, heartfelt "grace before meals" to share with the family tonight.

Dear Julia

Over the years I've written lots of long letters to my children for various reasons. My children need to know what's on my mind and in my heart. Like this one:

Dear Julia,

The summer you were twelve, you changed from a temperamental sixth-grader into a lovely, blossoming teenager on her journey toward womanhood. That summer you lost three teeth, grew two inches, started standing up straight, got your hair cut and permed, had your ears pierced, started earning your own money babysitting, lost five pounds, and learned to dive.

Now that you're fourteen, the physical changes are more subtle, but your emotional growth and maturity level are wonderful things to behold. I don't even mind shopping with you anymore. Remember the battles? You wanted the best brand names because they were "in" at school and I, being practical and frugal, refused to give in to the label wars? But now that you're earning most of your own spending money, it's fun to watch you look for bargains and good value.

You are such a good person. You're much more open with me than I was with my mother. Thank you for your love. Many girls your age don't kiss their parents good-night. But I'm glad you do, and happy you do it with such verve and sincerity. You make me feel loved!

I love you!

Mom

By the way, Julia is now thirty-two years old and writing letters and notes to her own three children.

The Stars in My Life

A star, though it seems magical at times, is nothing more than a self-luminous, self-contained, relatively stationary mass of gas, visible at night from Earth. And yet, if we look closely, we can always find a star twinkling a little faster and shining a little brighter that can light our way, as the star of Bethlehem did for the wise men two thousand years ago.

This coming year I'm going to try harder to appreciate the real "stars" in my life:

My neighbor, who offers to drive me somewhere.

My friend, who listens to my heart and
   asks nothing in return.
My father, who builds yet another
   beautiful object for my home.
My children, who take the time to
   explain something with infinite
   patience.

Why don't we make up a list of the stars
in our lives, send them a star-shaped
thank-you note, and let them know how
much we appreciate the way they light up
our lives?

A Minister's Challenge

It had been one of those weeks. Rain every
day. Too much to do, not enough time. The
older children snapped at me, I snapped at
them.

At church that Sunday our minister chal-
lenged, "Each time someone hurts you,
snubs you, is unkind to you or puts you
down, give that person a compliment that
same day."

Give that person a compliment? I thought.
Impossible!

By midweek life was so grumpy, I decided to give it a try.

I left my older son Michael, the talkative

one, a note: "Thanks for making your bed. Your room looks great!"

The next time Andrew threw a temper tantrum I scooped him off the floor, told him I loved him and read him a story.

When the girls were complaining about chores, I changed the subject. "You girls sure are good baby-sitters. Two people have told me this week how good you are with children."

You've probably figured out what happened next. Michael actually gave me a spontaneous hug on his way to catch the school bus the next day. Julia offered to watch Andrew, so I could go shopping by myself. Andrew asked me if he could help set the table for supper. And Jeanne invited me to go to a high-school musical with her.

Keeping Quiet

When my son Michael and his bride Amy returned from their honeymoon, they stayed at our house before moving to the town where Michael would be working as the director of a high-school band.

One night Amy, who'd been giving Michael haircuts all through college, said, "Don't you need a haircut, honey?"

Michael, who was getting ready for two weeks of active duty with the Wisconsin National Guard, said, "I think I'll get a haircut at the barber tomorrow."

Trying to be the frugal wife, Amy said, "Michael, that's ten dollars! I'll do it."

We all went out to the patio. Amy started clipping; Michael started grumbling; I was watching.

Michael began: "Put that other attachment on the clippers! You're going to make it too short."

"No, I'm not. This is the attachment I always use."

"No, it isn't. You're not going to get it right."

Oh no, I thought, *their first marital fight.*

"You wouldn't talk to the barber like that. Why can't you be nice and just tell me how you want it?"

"I'd be happy to tell the barber what I want, but you won't let me go."

At first, I wanted to side with Michael. *Maybe he should have gone to the barber. She's obviously not cutting it the way he likes.* Then I was on Amy's side. *She's trying so hard and she's doing a great job. Why can't he just appreciate her efforts?*

But something, a guardian angel on my shoulder, perhaps, kept me from speaking any of those thoughts. Instead, I changed the subject to break the tension and before long, all three of us were chatting like old friends.

Before supper that night, Michael scooped Amy into his arms, apologized profusely and told her it was one of the best haircuts he'd ever had. He promised never to complain again when she got out the clippers.

Wise Words

I'm not sure if it's because I wrote radio commercials that forced me to get a whole message across in thirty seconds of precious air time, or if it's because I just like bits of wisdom that come in small packages, but I've been a collector of sayings all my life. I snip them out of magazines, newsletters and church bulletins, and keep them in a folder. Sometimes I memorize them so I can pass them on to my children. Often I'll tape them to the front of the envelope of a letter I'm sending, hoping that all the mail carriers from here to there will enjoy the words of wisdom as well. They're also taped to my computer and on the walls of my home office.

Here are a few examples of my favorites:

We don't laugh because we feel good.
We feel good because we laugh.

No matter how long you nurse a
    grudge,
it won't get better.

If you must speak ill of another, do not
    speak it;
write it in the sand near the water's edge.

Over the years I learned that other people's wisdom in the form of sayings helped me, as a parent, make a point without belaboring the issue. During Andrew's sophomore year, when he missed getting his swim team letter by three points, I taped this one on his mirror: "Success is not permanent . . . and neither is failure." To encourage my daughter Julia to take good care of herself and her daughter while Julia was struggling through her divorce, I sent this one: "In life, the destination will take care of itself if the journey is done well."

Bifocals, Dentures and Hearing Aids

In my family it happens at age forty-two. Reading glasses. When my dad turned forty-two, he got them. Two years later, at age forty-two, my mom got them. And when I turned forty-two, I was no different.

Before I turned forty-three, I noticed my knees started cracking every time I walked upstairs. Then my left shoulder ached whenever the humidity rose. Not long after that, Andrew announced, "You sure do have a lot of gray hairs on top, Mom."

My mother said it best when she recited her favorite poem shortly after she got her first pair of reading glasses:

> *I can see through my bifocals,*
> *My dentures fit me fine.*
> *My hearing aid does wonders,*
> *But, Lord, I miss my mind!*

I laughed with her when she recited it years ago, and now that I've reached middle age myself, I've decided to keep my mother's sense of humor about it. I've also added this to my favorite quotes about aging: "Age is a matter of mind. If you don't mind, it doesn't matter."

Treasures of Love

In my bedroom I have two wooden plaques, a hand mirror and a small box, all etched with a wood-burning tool and hand-painted by my grandmother in the early 1900s. Minta Pearl Barclay Knapp was a college physics and math professor during a time when most women didn't even finish high school. She died in 1932, long before I was born. In spite of her amazing educational success, it's the objects she crafted in her spare time with her own hands that are her legacy to me.

I, too, have taken up a craft hobby in the past years with the hope that I can pass a bit of my creative self on to my children, grandchildren and friends. I save glass jars, the kind pickles, olives, bouillon cubes and mustard come in, and paint them with puffy fabric paint. They're colorful, fun to hold because of the puffy texture and quite lovely, if I do say so myself. I've filled my puffy paint jars with tea, candy, paper clips, cotton swabs or loose change, and given away more than five hundred of them to relatives, close friends and acquaintances.

Friends ask, "Why don't you sell them at craft fairs?"

I answer, "I do sell a few of them, but I never get back the value of my time. Besides, they're meant for people I love . . . people to whom I want to give the gift of my time and creativity."

Of course, I have to admit that I hope a few of my jars stand the test of time as my grandmother's wooden objects have, so that someday in the 2100s someone will say, "Mommy, where did this colorful jar come from?"

Pass It On

The temperature was five below zero. The icy wind caught my hat and sent it tumbling across the snowdrifts. Now the car wouldn't start. Not a grind or a grumble; the battery was dead.

My head dropped to the steering wheel. I prayed for a way out of the cold mess. Finally, I got out of the car and raised the hood. A few minutes later a man walked over to my car.

"Battery dead?" he said with a smile.

"Yes, sir. I left the lights on," I said sheepishly.

"No problem. I've got jumper cables. I'll have you up and running in no time."

Within minutes the engine purred to life. I thanked the man and offered him some money. "No thanks. But maybe you can help somebody else someday."

The very next day I was in a shoe store at a nearby shopping mall. Over the store loudspeaker I heard, "If anyone in the store has jumper cables, there's a family on the far side of the parking lot who needs help."

I didn't want to leave the warm store, walk clear across the parking lot, and stand there in the icy cold while strangers drained the electricity in my car and put it into their own. But then I remembered my cold, frightening experience the previous day. *Maybe you can help somebody else someday.*

When I reached the stranded car, a man, a woman and three children were huddled inside trying to keep warm. The woman jumped out, shook my hand and asked if they could pay me for the use of my brand-new jumper cables, purchased that very morning. I smiled. "No, but maybe you can help somebody else someday."

"It's a deal!" she exclaimed as her husband started their car.

Chapter Nine

Post-Party Cleanup
Age Gracefully and
Stay Young at Heart

Now we rejoice in our wonderful
new relationship with God —
all because of what our Lord Jesus Christ
has done in dying for our sins —
making us friends of God.
ROMANS 5:11 (TLB)

When the party's over and everyone has gone home, there comes a lull — a moment to reflect on the celebration. It's also time to clean up the mess and put things away in their proper place.

In "Post-Party Cleanup," Patricia Lorenz takes stock of her life and thinks about the people and events that have helped her to age gracefully and stay young at heart. She learns to forgive her ex-husband and, with their son, grieve his death and move forward. Pat witnesses the hectic work lives of her neighbors, which helps put her choices in perspective, and she cleans out her closets! Less is more, she learns, as she gets older.

Join Pat in the quiet of the party's aftermath and marvel at all that's been.

Under a Shade Tree . . .

When my ex-husband died in 1989, our young son Andrew (then age nine) was devastated. Even though Andrew and I attended the wake and funeral, we weren't able to go to the burial, which was held at Harold's boyhood hometown in southern Illinois, seven hours away from our home in Wisconsin.

All year Andrew talked about wanting to see his father's grave. I had never been one to visit graves, and I wasn't sure why he needed or wanted to see it. But finally, in August 1990, Andrew and I made the trip.

The little cemetery was out in the country on a hilltop, surrounded on all four sides by cornfields. The smell of wild clover, the sound of birds singing as they flew among the enormous oak trees and the warm summer breeze filled our senses. When we found Harold's grave marker, Andrew and I stood there, arms around each other, while Andrew talked aloud to his dad. Then Andrew and I talked together, recalling many special memories we had of his father. Finally, I asked my young son to sit quietly with me under a shade tree and to concentrate on locking that peaceful scene into his memory so he could always recall his father's final resting place.

That day I learned why people visit graves. It's a powerful way to get back in touch with the deceased. It opens up a flood of warm memories . . . and some therapeutic tears as well. It's also a way to share the message of life eternal with our children.

I'm going to take my son with me to visit

the graves of my mother and grandparents. The cemetery is the perfect setting for talking about what happens to our bodies when we die and for sharing with our children that powerful message of Christ's Resurrection.

A Time and Place for Prayer

It's seven o'clock on a May morning, seventy degrees in Oak Creek, Wisconsin. I'm sitting in a very comfortable yellow rocker on my deck with a large mug of Earl Grey tea. Two squirrels are dining on the ear of corn attached to the "squirrel diner" at the end of the deck and a dozen birds are singing their way through breakfast, also provided by the management.

This deck is my place and time for prayer. No newspapers, books, people or phone calls. Just me, the birds, squirrels and God.

Morning prayers were part of my life as a child. From first through twelfth grades, the Sisters of Loretto orchestrated morning prayers at school. But then in college and into marriage and motherhood, my morning prayers fell by the wayside. Twenty-five years passed.

Then one spring I discovered how quiet

and peaceful it was on my deck in the early morning, and I began to pray. I thanked God for this place of beauty and this hour of quiet and for this wonderful chair I found at a yard sale. I praised Him for the trees . . . and asked Him for many favors.

Do you have a specific place and a definite time for morning prayer? Believe me, it's an amazing way to start your day. It calms you, keeps your life focused, reminds you of what's truly important and begins each day on a positive, happy note. Promise yourself thirty minutes alone in your favorite spot every morning. Bring a cup of tea or coffee and perhaps the book of Psalms to get you started.

Taking Stock

When we take a break from our working lives, let's think about why it is we're working, and whether we're working too much or not enough, and whether we're doing our job well.

Years ago my neighbor dropped her first-grader off at my house every morning at 6:40 to wait for his school bus so that she had time to drop her preschooler off at the babysitter's and then drive the twenty miles to her job that began at 7:30. Her husband had a good-paying job from 8:00 a.m. to 5:00 p.m., but he went to bed early so that he could go to his moonlighting job from 2:00 a.m. till 7:00 a.m.

I wonder if these friends weren't laboring too hard. Where was the time for a long walk? Some relaxed talk? A leisurely bedtime story with the children? A family picnic? Alone time?

When I became a single parent, I decided that even though I could use the extra money that a full-time job would bring, my most important job was raising my four children. I decided to tighten the budget and continue to work part-time, and I've never regretted it.

Is it time for you to take inventory of how hard you work and why? Maybe a change in your work habits will make all the hosts of heaven and earth proclaim, "Here lived a great worker who did her job well and still had time to enjoy life."

Those Who Wipe Their Feet . . .

I used to get aggravated by telephone solicitors who call at all hours of the day and night to try to talk you into buying new siding for your home, or having your rugs shampooed, or purchasing tickets to some event or another. For years I'd try to figure out ways to do them in. Sometimes I'd just hang up. Other times I'd put the telephone on the table without hanging it up and let them talk on and on until they finally realized I wasn't there anymore.

But then I read about a woman who had worked at the Kremlin in Moscow for sixty years. When she retired, she was asked what she thought about all the different Communist leaders who had worked there. She explained simply that they could be divided into two groups, "Those who wiped their feet at the door and those who didn't."

After I read that, I decided to treat every person who called me with more respect. After all, they had to make a living, and if that work involved calling people at home, so be it. Now when I get an unwanted call, I usually say something like, "I'm sorry I can't take advantage of your offer, but I hope you have a great evening and make lots of sales."

It's interesting how much nicer you feel when you hang up after a call like that. I bet my blood pressure is lower these days, too.

Pitch In and Do It

Whose Job Is It?

This is the story about four people named Everybody, Somebody, Anybody *and* Nobody. *There was an important job to be done so everybody was sure somebody would do it. Anybody could have done it, but nobody did it. Somebody got angry about that because it was everybody's job. Everybody thought anybody could do it, but nobody realized that everybody wouldn't do it. It ended up that everybody blamed somebody when nobody did what anybody could have done.*

— *Author unknown*

How many times have I ignored a job that needed to be done simply because it was not my assigned task? How many times have I allowed myself to get upset because no one in the family emptied the dishwasher, or picked up the newspaper scattered all over the living room, or folded the laundry piled high on my bed?

If we approach daily tasks with the idea that it doesn't matter whether the job belongs to *Everybody, Somebody, Anybody or Nobody* — that instead what matters is the job gets done — then perhaps we'd be more apt just to pitch in and do it right then and there.

Today, let's find one task that's really not our job and do it anyway, with a smile and without expecting any gratitude. And tomorrow let's find another chore that needs to be done and do it. If it gets to be a habit, just imagine what we can accomplish in a year's time!

A Prayer for Smokers

One day at my job as a copywriter for a radio station in Milwaukee, Wisconsin, I had to write an ad for the Freedom from Smoking Center. Some of the copy information included a list of things every smoker gets absolutely free with every pack of cigarettes. Things like dirty ashtrays, sore throats, smelly fingers, possible heart attacks, chronic headaches, tobacco in your pockets, raspy voice, high blood pressure, chest pains, stained teeth, coughs, holes in your clothing, bad breath, emphysema, burning eyes, fatigue, shortness of breath, gum disease, bronchitis and lung cancer.

Goodness, I thought, *what a devastating list!* Although I'm not a smoker, I remembered my smoking friends, acquaintances and co-workers who had to fight all those negative things.

And so a prayer for them, and others: *Lord, help me to be especially considerate of those people who are trying to give up smoking or other bad habits. They need Your help.*

Tuesday Afternoons at Lucy's

Another scribbled, desperate note. I was starting to hate those little communications from my mother.

"Tell Pat to have Jeanne's birthday party without me," the note said. "I don't want to be there in this condition and spoil things for either of them."

Just a year before, my mother, fifty-six, and Dad, fifty-eight, had been having the time of their lives.

"Get a baby-sitter, Pat, and come skiing with us," Mother had invited joyfully. That winter they blasted their way down our northern Illinois snow-packed hills every week during their downhill ski lessons.

"We're finally learning to do the fox-trot the right way," Mom chuckled when I asked how their ballroom dancing classes were going.

Mom and Dad both worked full-time, but now that my younger sister was in college they eagerly planned their retirement. "We may tour the South Pacific!" Dad beamed.

"And take a trip to New England," Mother chirped. In the meantime, they partied, took weekend trips and enjoyed the good life with their close-to-retirement friends.

Then that same winter disaster struck like a monster eager to spoil everything. Amyotrophic lateral sclerosis (also known as Lou Gehrig's disease), which causes progressive muscle weakness, paralysis and eventual death, took root in Mother's body.

During the next few months she resorted first to a cane, then a walker and was finally confined to a wheelchair. Now, less than a year after the diagnosis, she was unable to move most of her muscles, barely able to swallow, unable to talk . . . and so depressed she was avoiding close family get-togethers, like her oldest granddaughter's birthday dinner.

And, oh, how Mother missed her friends, her job and her church activities. Knowing the disease was fatal, as her symptoms increased, she sank deeper into depression. She felt so useless, unable to wash her face or even comb her hair.

An intelligent woman who loved to read, she didn't have the strength to hold a book. We tried reading to her and even checked out books on records for the blind at the library, but she tired quickly of "listening" to books.

Mother's frustrations mounted until all she could do was cry and scribble those pathetic notes. I was tormented. *What can I do to help her out of this black mood?*

Her friends were also bewildered. "Pat, what can we do for your mother? We know it tires her out when we visit."

Her friend from the card club she'd been in for twenty-five years said, "We're praying for Lucy every day, but we want to do more. Can't you think of something?"

From her co-workers: "We miss your mother at school so much, but we're afraid if we visit she'll get too frustrated when she tries to talk."

Betty, one of Mom's closest friends, said, "I miss talking to Lucy on the phone every week. I want to see her, hold her hand. How can we make her more comfortable, more aware of our support?"

Help! I thought. Suddenly it wasn't just a problem of what I could do for my mother; now I was expected to come up with a solution for all her friends as well.

Betty stopped by my house one afternoon. "Pat, your mother has always looked to Mary, Jesus' mother, for help and comfort. Have you ever listened closely to the words of the 'Hail Mary'?"

Betty repeated it slowly. " 'Hail Mary, full of grace. The Lord is with thee. Blessed art thou among women and blessed is the fruit of thy womb, Jesus. Holy Mary, mother of God, pray for us sinners, now, and at the hour of our death. Amen.'

"Don't you see, Pat? 'Pray for us . . . now and at the hour of our death.' It's a beautiful prayer, so appropriate for your mother. Let's invite all your mother's friends to her house once a week to say the Rosary. We'll storm heaven with 'Hail Marys' and 'Our Fathers.' "

I pictured a crowd of mother's friends, relatives, co-workers, neighbors and fellow church members at her house. So many people at one time. *Will it be too much for her?* I wondered.

"Betty, let's send each person a letter of invitation and explain that the prayer sessions will have to be short — forty-five minutes or an hour, including visiting time, not long enough to tire Mom out, yet enough time for her to soak up the love her friends are aching to give. We'll start with the Rosary, then say whatever prayers we feel in our hearts. Afterward, each of us can stop by her wheelchair for a hug and a few words."

Betty made forty copies of the letter and mailed them out. The "Tuesday Afternoon Prayers at Lucy's" began in the spring of 1979 and continued each week through the summer months.

How Mother looked forward to those days! Each Monday she'd give me a note, "Pat, would you please set my hair tonight? Tomorrow my friends are coming." Until then she hadn't seemed to care how she looked.

She started wheeling herself around the house in her electric wheelchair, making sure one of us would pick up this and that . . . getting her home ready for her friends.

Another time a note said, "I could use a few new summer blouses. Pretty ones, cotton, easy to get on, bright prints."

As the Tuesday prayer sessions continued, Mother's mood brightened along with those bright blouses. She was simply awed by the number of people who came each week. Her whole attitude was changing. Were our Tuesday prayers being answered?

One Tuesday before the people were due

to arrive, Mother scribbled a note. "Pat, I'm sorry I can't come out today. With close friends and relatives, my face and throat react, making me feel exhausted and helpless. But as I sit in the den I will know that their love is here."

Less than a month after she wrote that note, Mother received Communion at home from our parish priest and then died quietly in the evening with my father at her side.

I'll never forget those Tuesday afternoons when thirty or forty people from all walks of life, some who didn't even know one another, crowded into my parents' home, knelt down on the floor and prayed for my mother. I'm sure most of us who knew and understood the finality of her disease were praying not that God would spare her life, but that He would ease her pain, restore her sense of self-worth and happiness, and surround her last weeks and days with the warmth of the love of God and the love of her friends.

God answered those prayers, every one of them. Even now, years later, Tuesday afternoons still have a way of reminding me of something very good that's going to happen to all of us after death. It's something that Mother knew about all along.

After she died I found this verse under-lined in her Bible: "Don't be troubled or afraid . . . I am going away, but I will come back to you again. If you really love me, you will be very happy for me, for now I can go to the Father, who is greater than I am" (John 14:27–28, TLB).

I believe those "Tuesday Afternoon Prayers at Lucy's" were a glorious reassur-ance. For her. For all of us.

Code to Live By

Maj. Bruce Swezey, a dear friend and neighbor who was a pilot with the Wisconsin Air National Guard, and I were talking about the various codes we live by. I asked, "What's your most important set of rules?"

Without blinking, Bruce said, "The thirty-six-word 'Emergency Action for Spin Recovery.'

Throttles: idle.
Rudder and ailerons: neutral.
Stick: abruptly full aft and hold.
Rudder: abruptly apply full rudder
    opposite spin direction and hold.
Stick: full forward one turn after
    applying rudder.
Control: neutral and recover from dive."

I laughed at Bruce's lightning-fast recital of this life-saving method of getting an airplane out of a downward spin. Then I shared with him the fifteen words that help me get more things accomplished in life. They help me find the answers to many problems. They help me communicate my real feelings to others. And they help me maintain a positive attitude no matter how much of a "spin" I am in.

My fifteen words?

> I am proud of you.
> What is your opinion?
> I love you.
> Thank you.
> Yes.

Rant and Rave, Rave and Rant

A national newspaper once noted that the Lord's Prayer contained fifty-six words, the Twenty-third Psalm 118 words, the Gettysburg Address 226 words and the Ten Commandments 297 words . . . while the U.S. Department of Agriculture directive on pricing cabbage weighed in at 15,629 words.

The Agriculture Department directive reminds me of the way I used to shout at my children when I thought they needed it.

First I ranted and raved, then I raved and ranted, usually repeating myself three or four times. Then, once again for emphasis but in a quieter, more adult tone, I recapped my sentiments, and finally summed it up with a "Do you understand?"

Of course they understood. They understood completely at the end of the first fifteen seconds. Was my fifteen-minute tirade really necessary? Of course not. One simple, calm "Mother Knows Best" directive would have done it . . . with a possible silent fifty-six word "Our Father" tucked on at the end.

Tough Love

"Hi, Mom. Bad news."

Oh, how I hated phone calls from my college student children that started that way! "What is it, Julia?"

"The check I wrote for my tuition bounced."

The rest of the conversation was one-sided, with me telling her in rather gruff tones that she simply had to start balancing her checkbook every month. She ended up in tears.

The next day I fussed and fumed. *Do I bail her out or let her learn from her mistake?*

I was so tormented that finally I decided to make the two-mile drive to Lake Michigan and try to think it out in the solitude I knew I would find there.

Two- to three-foot waves crashed loudly against the sand under immense white clouds. I walked close to the water, skittering back each time a wave rolled up close to my sneakers. Suddenly, one caught me off guard and soaked my shoe, sock and pant leg, making me quite uncomfortable in the fifty-degree weather. From then on I walked farther away from the shoreline. I'd learned my lesson!

And I had found my answer. Julia, too, had been caught off guard. Perhaps if she had to "walk with wet feet" for a month at college by living without spending money, she'd learn a lot more about financial responsibility. She could use the money from her part-time job to make good on her tuition check. It would be uncomfortable, but sometimes that's the only way we'll learn.

Dear Julia, I thought as I made my way back to the car, *I love you. Try to understand.*

A Scary Situation

One of the most frightening times of my life happened on the way home to Wisconsin from Kentucky. I was driving my beautiful, eighteen-year-old niece Kirstie and my fourteen-year-old son Andrew home after visiting my brother and his family in Louisville for a week. Andrew was asleep in the backseat when, near Chicago, I had to change highways. Unfortunately, I got off the interstate at the wrong exit and ended up on a deserted, dead-end, dirt-and-gravel road. I turned around, got back on the main highway and tried to get off again, only to end up at the same spot.

This time as I got off, I noticed a car following me. Quickly, I made a U-turn just as the other car sped up and pulled alongside me. Five or six jeering men started to get out of the car. Terrified, I locked my car door and gunned the engine, spewing dust and rocks behind me. I raced back toward the interstate, praying like gangbusters, drenched in fear. Five minutes later the right exit appeared and we headed home, out of danger.

For the next hour of the trip I said prayers of thanksgiving and took lots of deep breaths. I recalled stories my dad told about his experiences as a World War II fighter pilot in the South Pacific. "Weren't you scared?" I'd ask. He'd say he just remembers flying one mile after another, trying not to think about what could happen, knowing that God was flying with him.

Whether we're facing an enemy in war, an ambush on a deserted road or struggling to make it through the next paycheck, if we have faith that God is there guiding us mile after mile, then we'll make it to safety.

Breaking the Stereotype

Someone once said that life is made up of:

> The tender teens
> The teachable twenties
> The tireless thirties
> The fiery forties
> The fretful fifties
> The serious sixties
> The sacred seventies
> The aching eighties
> Shortening breath
> Death, Sod, God.

It all sounds so neat and orderly, doesn't it? But when I first heard this little version

258

of the stages of life, I was in my late thirties, which hadn't been tireless at all. In fact, with four young children and various part-time jobs, I'd been exhausted most of the time.

When I was in my "fiery forties," believe me, there were days I didn't feel fiery at all. Most days, in fact.

What's fretful about the fifties? Neither I nor any of my friends in their fifties are fretful . . . tireless, perhaps, and other times aching with exhaustion from working and playing so hard.

A dear friend in her sixties is quite teachable as she takes one college course after another in her spare time.

And a favorite aunt in her seventies is seriously enjoying life and friends, and discovering new things from her numerous grand nieces and nephews, who also enjoy her fiery enthusiasm for life.

The white-haired octogenarian down the block who just retired is as fiery as they come, actively involved in politics, especially issues concerning the elderly.

It's a fact to be accepted and treasured: We can all be exactly what we want to be at *any* stage in life.

Less Is More

One thing about being single and an empty-nester is that you get to fill up all the closets. No sharing; every inch is mine. And what happens over the years is you end up with far too many clothes. I have clothes for every season, every reason, every style, size and event.

I should take my cue from my step-mother Bev who, at age seventy-nine, always looks like she just stepped out of a fashion magazine. When it comes to clothes, she's a minimalist. For instance, for summer wear she has five or six really nice spotless T-shirts; I have about thirty. Some are in the same condition as my dad's shop rags. How can you ever get rid of the T-shirt your daughter painted in high school? Or the one you bought at the Eiffel Tower? Or the one your son bought you for Mother's Day fifteen years ago?

Well, I'm going to try. My goal for this year is to reduce my clothes-chaos from three full closets to perhaps one and a half. I'm going to try to find something that looks really good on me and stick with that style. I'm going to give the rest away to Goodwill or Human Concerns so that others who have little can have more. I'm going to share a few special things with friends who, unlike me and my dreams, have already lost the extra twenty pounds.

Yes, I am going to conquer my closets! My new mantra: Less is more.

I feel lighter already.

One Step at a Time

It was a beautiful spring day, but I didn't feel joyous as I surveyed the terrible mess of my yard. Bare muddy spots, overgrown bushes, weeds all over the place, and a lawn that either had to be mowed or used for pasture. I thought, *It's hard being responsible for everything around the house, inside and out.*

I decided to tackle the mowing first, but when I pulled the lawn mower out of winter storage, I discovered that the gas can was empty. Then I saw a sign on the mower that said, "Check oil before starting engine." I couldn't even find the oil gauge.

I felt frustrated at not being able to do the simplest job on my list, so I called a neighbor for help. He and his family were in the midst of a party for their son. I apologized for interrupting them and quickly hung up the phone.

Then the tears came unbidden. I felt very alone and scared. I stopped sniffling when I realized that it wasn't making me feel any better. "Dear Lord, what do I do now?"

I thought to call another neighbor . . . and she gave me a quick lesson in lawn mower maintenance and loaned me some gas. Two hours later, after cutting the lawn, pulling weeds and trimming bushes, I was dripping wet from perspiration and totally exhausted, but somehow feeling better than I had in months.

You may be facing an overwhelming situation, but please realize that you can do for today *one thing* to move you toward your goal. Remember, one day at a time, one step at a time — and you'll get there.

Never Too Late

September — school is starting and we'll all be changing our routines somewhat. *Ah ha,* the perfect time to start a new habit! How about an exercise habit?

Before my youngest child Andrew left for college, I'd get up at 6:15 a.m. each school day and jump into my casual clothes and walking shoes. I'd fix Andrew's breakfast and my tea. We'd enjoy thirty minutes together while he ate and got ready. Then, as soon as he was out the door at 7:05 a.m., I'd take off walking. Fast walking, mind you. Even though Andrew's out of school now, my walking habit is still with me, at least on some days. Most days I jump on my bike for a long ride.

Sometimes I wear a radio headset that is tuned to the oldies station. All those great rock and roll tunes of the fifties, sixties and seventies keep me moving fast. In between the tunes I hear the news. Often, I leave the radio at home and meditate, plan my day, or just commune with nature on the beautiful bike path along the creek just two blocks from my house. It's a great way to start the morning. Half an hour later, I return home, shower, eat breakfast and head for my home office. That's *my* exercise routine.

Now let me tell you about Anne Clark's exercise habit. She competed in more than five hundred races worldwide and was the proud owner of more than thirty age-related records in races that ranged from short 5Ks to marathons. What's so unusual about that, you say? Nothing, except for the fact that Anne didn't start running until she was sixty-nine years old and at age eighty-seven she was still running races. Anne said that running cured her age-related aches and pains, including back pain, arthritis and bursitis. To look at her sleek physique and rosy complexion, you'd have thought she was in her early sixties.

When I read about people like Anne Clark, it reminds me that God meant for our bodies to remain young and healthy well into old age. But we have to do our part. The good news is it's never too late to begin a fitness habit. Let's start today . . . for the rest of our lives.

While the Sun Comes Up

It was a dilemma I hadn't expected. On the day before the second anniversary of my ex-husband's death, our eleven-year-old son Andrew came to me with an odd request for honoring his memory.

"Mom, I've got it all planned," Andrew said. "I want you and me to go out to the lake, and sit and think about Dad while the sun comes up. We'll take along cherry Jell-O with sliced bananas in it. That's what Dad liked. We used to make it when I'd see him on weekends. Okay, Mom?"

It wasn't exactly okay. I still had hurt feelings about Harold. I was still bitter about the way our marriage had ended, how he'd filed for the divorce without any effort at marriage counseling, how he'd remarried the week our divorce was final. No, this would be too awkward.

"Andrew, it's October. It's supposed to be really cold tomorrow. Couldn't you just think about your dad at home?"

"Mom, please. We can wear long underwear and take a blanket."

I thought I'd done a good job of helping Andrew adjust to his father's death, and I was determined to be the best "only" parent a child could have. But I was unprepared for something like this. As Andrew waited for my reply, the pleading look on his face told me how much this would mean to him.

"All right, Andrew. We'll have to get up at five-fifteen if you want to get there while it's still dark."

"No problem, Mom! I'll set my alarm. Do you think Wayne would come if I asked him?"

I wondered what Wayne, the man I'd been dating for three months, would think about Andrew's plan. Wayne's wife had died just two months after Harold, and I was sure that Wayne was still dealing with his own grief. I didn't know if it was fair to drag him along to Andrew's strange beach ceremony.

That afternoon, when Wayne stopped by

the house, Andrew explained his plan and said he'd like the three of us to be together. "So, Wayne, do you want to go?"

I shot Wayne a look that said something like "Are you sure about this?" Then I said, "Do you realize it's going to be only twenty degrees tomorrow morning? With the wind off the lake, the windchill factor will probably be below zero!"

Wayne smiled. "Sure I want to go, Andrew. I'm glad you asked me."

Wayne arrived at our house at 5:40 the next morning, wearing full winter gear. I was wearing a jogging suit under my clothes, plus a heavy jacket and earmuffs. The Jell-O Andrew had made was retrieved from the refrigerator and the container put in a brown paper bag. Wayne tossed an old green bedspread into the van.

A few minutes later, in the pitch-darkness, we arrived at Grant Park Beach in South Milwaukee, the only humans in sight. Wayne and Andrew smoothed out the bedspread on the sand, about thirty feet from the jet-black water. We moved up close to the front of the bedspread and pulled the back half up around us as a windbreak.

Andrew had instructed us carefully beforehand that we would sit without talking. At first his silence rule made me uncomfortable. But then I looked at Wayne and Andrew and knew that they were both remembering and missing the person they had loved so much in life.

I knew Wayne was thinking about the wonderful relationship he'd had with Janet, his wife of thirty-one years. And without a doubt, Andrew was thinking about Harold, about the walks they often took along this lake, about the plays and concerts his father had taken him to.

I recalled the early days of our marriage. The bike rides, teaching Harold to ice-skate, the two wonderful trips to Arizona to visit his sister and brother and their families.

I remembered when Andrew was born, in Harold's fifty-first year, and how proud he was of his new son. Why, he'd passed out cigars the day he found out I was pregnant!

I remembered how scared I was when Harold had emergency gallbladder surgery. And how I laughed when he dressed up in a crazy red plaid sport coat and too short orange plaid pants for "Nerd Day" at the high school where he was principal.

Suddenly the unhappy times in our marriage faded away, and as I watched a new line of pink-and-steel-blue clouds inching their way onto the horizon, I felt as if a dam had broken. All the good memories I'd buried the day Harold moved out of our home came rushing back.

I pulled the bedspread tighter around my neck and snuggled closer to Andrew, who had his head on my chest, trying to keep the cold away. The more I thought about Harold, the more I realized how much I missed him.

Even though it was still twenty minutes or so until sunrise, the intensity of sunlight from below the horizon was starting to fill the beach with an eerie sense of "almost" day. And I was being filled with an eerie sense of "almost" peace.

Andrew motioned that it was time to eat the Jell-O. I took the lid off the container. When I placed one of the plastic spoons into Wayne's hand, I squeezed his fingers through the bulky gloves. He smiled, and I knew he understood what was going on in my mind and in Andrew's.

So we ate cherry Jell-O at dawn on the shore of Lake Michigan in a windchill that felt very close to zero degrees. But somehow I wasn't shivering. And the Jell-O tasted good.

Just as the sun popped up on the horizon in a magnificent display of color, Wayne and Andrew stood up.

"It's okay to talk now," Andrew said.

Wayne put his big arms around Andrew and held him close. "I know what you're going through, son. I loved my wife very much, just like you loved your dad. And it's a wonderful thing to take the time to cherish those memories. And, Andrew, I don't think I told you how much I love cherry Jell-O with bananas!"

I stood up as the full ball of wild orange sun now rested precariously and breathtakingly beautiful above the horizon, and I said, "Andrew, let's walk along the shore for a minute."

"Good idea," Wayne said. "I'll go warm up the van."

So it was that Wayne and I were able to let an eleven-year-old child lead us into a strange world of ceremony and silence . . . and where we all, especially me, were able to grieve openly. Andrew and I faced the love we had for Harold Lorenz head-on and then moved ahead in a celebration of life that included new love and wonderful warm feelings.

The Gift of Hope

I took a walk on the beach one morning. As I scuffled along in the sand, roaring waves crashed so loudly it made me wonder how many decibels of sound they create. Lake Michigan is so mighty that it looks, sounds and feels like the ocean. I winked at the handsome lifeguard on duty, my seventeen-year-old son Andrew, who smiled but only said a few words because lifeguards aren't supposed to talk with beach patrons.

In my heavy running shoes I plowed through the sand, thinking about life. Three of my friends were in turmoil. One had been advised to see a surgeon immediately after a bad mammogram. Another, who was being promoted to captain for the local airline, had been told his partner had failed the exam and had been fired. Another friend had just separated from his wife and moved three hours away, leaving their seven-year-old without his father on a regular basis. I was also in turmoil, knowing this was Andrew's last school year before leaving home for college. I was already feeling the empty nest and aching.

As the noisy waves crashed on the sand and soaked my shoes, I was reminded of the gift of hope. With hope I can be eternally optimistic. When I get sick, I have hope that I'll get better. When I lose a job, the gift of hope buoys me through the hunt for the next one. When I'm separated from a loved one, the gift of hope keeps me moving forward, one step at a time, toward a new life.

Like the waves at my feet, the gift of hope returns again and again to carry me like a boat on the water to safer territory. Hope is the cushion that keeps me sane when the waves crash down upon me. What a marvelous treasure, this gift of hope!

Ale 10/05
HV 9/08
TH 1/12
cm 8/16
TH 4/17
Cm 11/17